D0947136

The Cult of the Prince Consort

The Cult of the
PRINCE CONSORT

Elisabeth Darby
Nicola Smith

Yale University Press
New Haven and London 1983

For Nick

Designed by Stephanie Hallin.
Set in Monophoto Bembo and printed in Great Britain by Butler & Tanner Ltd, Frome, Somerset.

Library of Congress Cataloging in Publication Data
Darby, Elisabeth
    The Cult of the Prince Consort.
    Includes bibliographical references and index.
    1. Albert, Prince Consort of Victoria, Queen of Great Britain, 1819–1861—Monuments, etc. I. Smith, Nicola.
II. Title.
DA559.A1S6   1983   941.081′092′4   83–42869
ISBN 0–300–03015–0

Contents

Acknowledgements

WE ARE GRATEFUL to Her Majesty the Queen for graciously allowing us to study and quote from material in the Royal Archives and for permission to reproduce photographs and works of art in the Royal Collection. We would like to thank Sir Robin Mackworth-Young for kindly reading the manuscript. Miss Jane Langton, Miss Elizabeth Cuthbert and Miss Frances Dimond of the Royal Archives helped us in many ways, freely sharing their extensive knowledge and offering invaluable suggestions. Sir Oliver and Lady Millar, and Mr. Geoffrey de Bellaigue kindly assisted us with enquiries about works of art in the Royal Collection, and we are also grateful to the Hon. Mrs. Jane Roberts and to Mrs. Charlotte Crawley for showing us material in the Print Room at Windsor Castle.

We are especially indebted to Nicholas Penny, Benedict Read and Michael Darby who discussed the subject with us on many occasions. Without their encouragement and support, this book would never have been written. We would also like to thank our colleagues in the Courtauld Institute of Art and the Department of the Environment, in particular Philip Ward-Jackson and Peter Curnow who assisted us with photographs. We are grateful to John Nicoll and Stephanie Hallin of Yale University Press for their help at all stages in the production of this book. Sarah Wimbush of the National Portrait Gallery Archive, and Amanda Herries at the Museum of London, kindly arranged for us to see items in their care, and the staff of many other institutions, museums, galleries, libraries and record offices promptly and fully answered our enquiries.

We are indebted to Cambridge University for permission to quote from its archive, to Lady Joan Worthington and to Mr. Richard A. Scott who generously allowed us to use manuscripts in their possession, and also to Sir Charles Hobhouse, Bart., for granting us permission to quote from manuscripts in the British Library. Quotations from correspondence between Queen Victoria and the Crown Princess of Prussia, first published in *Dearest Mama*, *Your Dear Letter* and *Darling Child* (all edited by Roger Fulford), are here reproduced by courtesy of Bell and Hyman. Part of Chapter Three first appeared in a Shorter Notice in the *Burlington Magazine*, vol. 123, no. 937, April 1981.

PHOTOGRAPHIC ACKNOWLEDGEMENTS

The following photographs are reproduced by gracious permission of Her Majesty the Queen: 2, 3, 4, 5, 6, 7, 8, 9, 12, 13, 14, 16, 17, 18, 20, 21, 23, 24, 25, 27, 28, 29, 30, 31, 33, 55, 56, 59, 68, 79, 87, 109. Grateful acknowledgement is made to the following for the supply of photographs and for permission to reproduce them: Birmingham City Engineer's

That he was much adored by all,
    These tablets to his worth declare,
Not only fixed on churches' wall,
    But raised around us everywhere,
      Great Britain through.
In peaceful hamlet taking form,
    Of school-house 'neath the spreading beech,
Which erst had sheltered from the storm,
    A ruder cot, with dame to teach,
      The wealthier few.
Fountains, and windows, seats, and parks,
    Towns of importance grant;
While cities erect still costlier marks,
    Substantial and elegant,
      Edificies of use.
These are memorials, manifest,
    For future age to see,
With what esteem we prized the blest,
    Of goodly memory—

J.B. Goodrich, *Memorial Poem on the Opening
    of the Albert Museum, Exeter*, Exeter, 1868.

Introduction

JOHN HOBHOUSE, Lord Broughton, woke up in his quiet country retreat on Monday, 16 December 1861 to discover 'The Papers in mourning—The Prince Consort *died* about eleven o'clock on Saturday night.'[1] It was a very great shock, to Lord Broughton and to the nation as a whole. Prince Albert of Saxe Coburg-Gotha was only forty-two and apparently had not been ill for long.[2] Since his marriage to Queen Victoria in 1840, he had become the mainstay of his wife and family and a respected and imaginative adviser to Government, although the people had mistrusted him as a foreigner and never really warmed to him. Lord Broughton noted sadly that the Prince 'was an excellent man in all the relations of life—but his merits were not generally acknowledged',[3] and he returned to the book he was currently reading. This was Thomas Carlyle's *On Heroes, Hero-Worship and the Heroic in History*,[4] and the enormous success of this series of essays hints at one reason why the popular acclaim which had eluded the Prince Consort in life was heaped upon his memory. Carlyle encouraged the cult of the individual, and promulgated the doctrine that 'Worship of a Hero is transcendent admiration of a Great Man . . . No nobler feeling than this of admiration for one higher than himself dwells in the breast of man.'[5] Queen Victoria had always been convinced of Prince Albert's qualities and she now buried herself amidst memorials of him—some simple and touching, some breathtakingly extravagant and some, to modern taste, macabre. She hoped that the people would worship him too. The fashion for extravagant mourning and the search for heroes got this cult off to a good start.

Moved also by genuine compassion for the widowed Queen (and by a sense of remorse which press obituaries instilled), the nation threw itself unhesitatingly into the gestures of grief. On the day of Prince Albert's funeral, London was described as being like 'a city struck by the Plague'[6] with 'all shops shut or partially so, and all private houses as much closed as if each owner had lost a near relative'.[7] The following Sunday people crowded into churches, 'covered with the symbols of mourning, to an extent which has never been exceeded',[8] to hear funeral sermons. As one writer remarked, 'No one wishes each other "a *merry* Xmas" this year.'[9] For some time thereafter people's attention was focused on suitable tributes and commemorative schemes. Few of the portrait photographs and prints, which could not be produced quickly enough in the weeks following the death, now survive and the numerous biographies today gather dust on the farthest library shelves, but the most conspicuous tributes—the various buildings, monuments and the army of statues erected to his memory—are still to be seen in towns throughout the country.

There is considerable irony in this for the profusion of monuments is the last thing that Prince Albert himself would have wanted. When in 1853 it was suggested that a memorial

1

1. Joseph Durham: Memorial of the Great Exhibition of 1851, South Kensington.

to the Great Exhibition of 1851 should incorporate a statue of himself in honour of the prominent part he had played in its success, the Prince wrote to Lord Granville in no uncertain terms: 'I can say, with perfect absence of humbug, that I would rather not be made the prominent feature of such a monument, as it would both disturb my quiet rides in Rotten Row to see my own face staring at me, and if (as is very likely) it became an artistic monstrosity, like most of our monuments, it would upset my equanimity to be permanently ridiculed and laughed at in effigy.'[10] The plan was accordingly dropped, and eventually it was decided that the principal figure should be that of Queen Victoria. The death of the Prince Consort in December 1861 changed the design again. Almost immediately, the Prince of Wales declared the Queen's wish that a statue of Prince Albert should replace her own, and conveyed his own desire to bear the cost of this. The figure was executed by Joseph Durham, and the monument was unveiled with great ceremony on 10 June 1863 (Plate 1).[11] By this date the enthusiasm for Albert memorial schemes throughout the country was at its height. The Queen's expressed wish (and the Prince of Wales's generosity) had set a far-reaching precedent.

2

1. 'A Sort of Religion'

WHEN Princess Alice called her mother back into the Blue Room at Windsor Castle where the Prince Consort lay suffering from typhoid fever on the evening of Saturday, 14 December 1861, Queen Victoria knew that death was at hand. At 10.50 p.m. Prince Albert died. Years later, in 1872, the Queen could still vividly recall how 'Two or three long but perfectly gentle breaths were drawn, the hand clasping mine and . . . *all*, *all*, was over . . . I stood up, kissed his dear heavenly forehead & called out in a bitter and agonising cry "Oh! my dear Darling!" and then dropped on my knees in mute, distracted despair, unable to utter a word or shed a tear! Ernest Leiningen & Sir C. Phipps lifted me up, and Ernest led me out . . .'[1] She returned to the death chamber twice the next day and wrote to her eldest daughter, the Crown Princess of Prussia, that Prince Albert appeared 'beautiful as marble— and the features so perfect, though grown very thin'. Although the body was not placed in the coffin until the 18th, Queen Victoria did not look upon it again, for, as she told her daughter, 'I felt I would rather (as I know He wished) keep the impression given of life and health than have this one sad though lovely image imprinted too strongly on my mind!'[2] Prostrate with grief, the Queen retired to Osborne on the 19th, unable to face the ordeal of the funeral service which was conducted in St. George's Chapel on the 23rd.

Queen Victoria had depended upon the Prince Consort in every way, from drafting her official letters and despatches, to approving her dresses and bonnets. Suddenly, her support was gone. In moments of extraordinary composure during the early days of her widowhood, fostered by a recollection of Prince Albert's advice at the time of her mother's death that she must control her feelings and not dwell on her sorrow, the Queen expressed her determination to carry out her duties to the country as he would have wished her to do. But these moments of calm resolution alternated with paroxysms of despair. Although she believed Prince Albert to have been 'too pure and too good for this world',[3] and that 'His great soul is *now only* enjoying *that* for which it *was* worthy',[4] it seemed at times that 'to live without him is really no life', and in these anguished moments, Queen Victoria's only wish was to 'follow him soon'.[5] She was consoled, however, by the conviction that, still 'living, only invisible',[6] her husband continued to watch over her, and that they would meet again in their 'eternal, real home'.[7] This expression might easily be taken for a cliché of mourning—but in this particular period it was susceptible to literal interpretation as never before or since. The Queen subscribed to the popular view which imagined heaven in the most sentimental and anthropomorphic terms.[8] In this she was encouraged by her Scottish chaplain, Norman Macleod, a prominent figure in the movement,[9] and more importantly, her belief had been ratified by Prince Albert himself.

After the death of her mother, the Duchess of Kent, in March 1861, the Queen and Prince Albert had read together Reverend William Branks's *Heaven our Home*, the first edition of which was sold out within a week of its publication in 1861, and which eventually sold over 100,000 copies. The author was emphatic that friends would meet again in an '*eternal home of love*, and *recognise* them, and *speak* with them in the *language of heaven*', and that those already departed have a '*deep* and *glowing* and *unquenchable* interest' in those still on earth.[10] Prince Albert had accepted these views, and expressed to his wife his certainty that they would 'recognise each other and be together in eternity'.[11] After his death the Queen compiled an *Album Inconsolativum* of letters of condolence, and of extracts from tracts concerning the future life and from the works of German and English poets.[12] Of these, Alfred Tennyson's *In Memoriam* seems to have afforded her particular consolation, and large sections of the work were transcribed into the *Album Inconsolativum*. The Queen there altered words to make their meaning more applicable to her own situation: she substituted 'widow' for 'widower', and 'her' for 'his' in the lines 'Tears of a Widower', for example.[13] She recorded in her diary for 5 January 1862 that she was 'much soothed and pleased with Tennyson's "In Memoriam"', and that 'only those who have suffered as I do, can understand these beautiful poems'.[14] The consolation afforded by Tennyson's *In Memoriam* was perhaps partly a result of Prince Albert's admiration for it, but also because of the belief it expresses in a future life. The Duke of Argyll informed Tennyson that the Queen found certain passages 'specially soothing' because they echoed her strong belief 'in the *Life presence* of the Dead', and it was for this reason too that he advised the Poet Laureate not to use the word 'late' in relation to the Prince Consort when he was invited to Osborne in April 1862.[15] The Queen also thanked the poet for his dedication to the *Idylls of the King* which Tennyson had written in response to a request from Princess Alice that he should 'idealise' her late father in verse. This 'soothed' Queen Victoria's 'aching, bleeding heart',[16] and was transcribed into the *Album Inconsolativum*. The last line of the dedication ('Till God's Love set thee at his side again') also held out the promise of a future life in which the couple would be reunited.

Reflecting her determination to 'treat him as living',[17] Queen Victoria ordered that the Prince's private rooms at Windsor, Balmoral and Osborne were to be retained just as he had left them, and kept up as if he were still to use them. When Lord Clarendon visited the Queen at Osborne in March 1862:

> She talked upon all sorts of subjects as usual and referred to the sayings and doings of the Prince as if he was in the next room. It was difficult to believe that he was not, but in his own room where she received me everything was set out on his table and the pen and his blotting-book, his handkerchief on the sofa, his watch going, fresh flowers in the glass, etc., etc., as I had always been accustomed to see them, and as if he might have come in at any moment.[18]

Every night Prince Albert's clothes were laid out, and a jug of hot water and clean towels were put in his dressing room, as though ready for his use.[19] Nevertheless, the truth was revealed by the coloured photograph of his corpse which hung over his side of the bed in each of the royal residences (Plate 2). This has now been replaced by one showing his effigy (Plate 3).

Queen Victoria also kept by her bedside casts of the Prince's face and hands which had

2. Queen Victoria's bedroom at Balmoral.

3. Coloured photograph of the effigy of Prince Albert, Osborne.

been taken by the sculptor William Theed.[20] Though she could not bring herself to look at the deathmask (knowing that Prince Albert had found such things distasteful),[21] the hands comforted her, and in moments of despair she clung to them as she might have done in life. The numerous painted and sculpted portraits of the dead Prince which Queen Victoria commissioned also provided her with solace, and served as the most vivid reinforcements to her belief that her husband was still watching over her.

During his lifetime, Queen Victoria had been guided by Prince Albert in artistic matters. After his death, she had to rely on what she knew to have been his taste and choice of artists, and on the judgement of close relatives. Of the latter, only the Prince of Wales was excluded. The previous autumn he had indulged in an indiscreet affair with an actress, and the Queen believed that worry over his son's 'fall' had contributed to the Prince Consort's death. In her distress, she could hardly bear Bertie's presence, and he was accordingly dispatched on a continental tour early in February 1862. Though he contributed to the financing of the Royal Mausoleum, the Prince of Wales did not assist his mother with her other memorial schemes. In the planning and execution of these, Queen Victoria relied especially on her two eldest daughters, and in particular on the Crown Princess of Prussia, her father's favourite, though she had been unable to rejoin her mother in England immediately for fear that the strain might endanger her pregnancy.

The Crown Princess had spent the day of her father's funeral in Berlin sitting 'with all dear, darling, blessed Papa's photographs on my knees, devouring them with my eyes, kissing them and feeling as if my heart would break'.[22] Queen Victoria sent her other 'dear precious relics and hair',[23] and later a drawing of her father's body by E.H. Corbould 'in a case with a key'.[24] Early in January 1862 she sent copies of the casts of Prince Albert's hands to the Crown Princess who described the anguish of unpacking them: 'It was a *dreadful moment* when I first saw them I thought my heart wd. break—I felt quite faint! They were the 1st thing that brought home to me the dreadful reality—those *dear hands* I was so happy to kiss so happy to hold—the rings I knew so well—all so like—and yet thin as I had never known him. Oh how dreadful to see them only in the cold plaster & to think I shall never kiss them again, it was an agony wh. I cannot describe!'[25] The Queen had, of course, intended to soothe rather than distress her daughter, and the Crown Princess later wrote that the casts 'are really a comfort to me!'[26] She also derived consolation from assisting her mother with ideas for memorial schemes. Queen Victoria had written to her on 18 December 1861, 'I do hope you will come in two or three weeks; it will be such a blessing then. I shall need your taste to help me in carrying out works to His memory which I shall want His aid to render at all worthy of Him! You know His taste. You have inherited it.'[27] The Crown Princess advised her mother on the design of the Royal Mausoleum, the Albert Memorial Chapel, and on the statues and busts which played such a prominent role in Queen Victoria's commemoration of her husband.

Ignoring the Prince Consort's request that should he die before her, she would not 'raise even a single marble image' to his name,[28] the Queen proceeded immediately after his death to commission two full-size statues, a group, and several busts and statuettes of her beloved husband for her residences, and as gifts for members of her family and faithful servants. In addition, photographs and several of the memorial paintings which Queen Victoria commissioned show her alone, or with her children, grouped around posthumous busts of the Prince Consort.

6

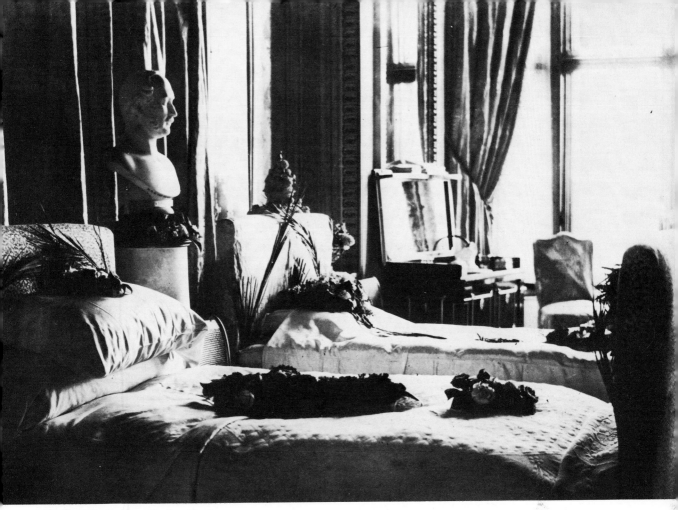

4. The Blue Room, Windsor Castle.

William Theed, a sculptor who had been respected by Prince Albert, was chosen to execute much of this memorial sculpture. The Queen retired to Osborne on 19 December 1861 and it was here, within two weeks of the Prince Consort's death, that Theed began work on the first posthumous bust. She told the Crown Princess on 27 January 1862 that it was 'life itself'.[29] The completed marble bust, showing the Prince Consort with bare shoulders, was placed between the two beds in the Blue Room at Windsor Castle where he had died, and which the Queen wanted to 'dedicate . . . to him not as a Sterbe-Zimmer—but as a living beautiful monument' (Plate 4).[30] The appearance of the room was recorded in photographs, and on the first anniversary of the Prince's death, Theed's bust was moved and placed on one of the beds where, surrounded by flowers, it formed the focus of the three memorial services which were conducted there that day.[31]

A second bust by Theed, also completed in 1862, shows Prince Albert with drapery over his left shoulder held by a buckle carrying a portrait of the young Queen Victoria (Plate 5). The pedestal for this, ornamented with cherubs' heads and flowers, was designed by Princess Alice, and took Theed twelve months to finish 'owing to the minuteness of execution'.[32] In February 1864[33] it was placed in the entrance hall at Osborne on a 'memorial altar'[34] of coloured marbles with bronze ormolu wreaths.

7

5. William Theed: Bust of Prince Albert, Osborne House.

6. Queen Victoria, the Crown Princess of Prussia, Princess Alice and Prince Alfred, Windsor Castle, 28 March 1862.

7. Queen Victoria and Princess Alice in mourning, 1862.

8. Albert Graefle: *Queen Victoria as a widow*, Royal Collection.

9. Joseph Noel Paton; Unfinished painting of Queen Victoria and her children grouped around a bust of Prince Albert, Royal Collection

Both busts appear, garlanded with wreaths, in photographs taken in 1862 of the Queen with her sons and daughters (Plates 6 and 7), or of the children on their own. The draped bust is also to be seen in the background of Albert Graefle's portrait of Queen Victoria as a widow (Plate 8), commissioned in 1863, and completed the following year,[35] and in the unfinished memorial picture of her with some of her children which the Scottish painter Joseph Noel Paton was summoned to Windsor in February 1863 to execute (Plate 9).[36] The Queen expressed some dissatisfaction with Princess Alice's pose and also her own ('there is no repose or sorrow about it')[37] in the initial sketches, but she found the pencil and water-colour studies which he made during the winter of 1863 '*most* beautiful'.[38] The Crown Princess thought that the composition was promising, as did her mother,[39] but the painting never proceeded much further. Paton himself found the subject morbid and was relieved to be excused from the commission on the grounds of ill-health.[40]

While at Windsor, Paton was commissioned to execute a second memorial picture. This showed the Blue Room in moonlight, with the figure of the Queen kneeling (as she did every night she stayed at the Castle) by the bed in which Prince Albert had died. Queen Victoria conceived the idea for this painting while looking at the illustrations by Noel Paton and his brother Waller Hugh Paton to W.E. Aytoun's *Lays of the Scottish Cavaliers*.[41] One of these, for the poem *The Widow of Glencoe*, is a moonlight scene showing the bereaved woman prostrate on the spot where her husband had been killed. This image of the sorrowing woman, so poignantly reminiscent of her own nightly ritual at Windsor, prompted Queen Victoria to commission the painting which, when it was completed in March 1864, she described as 'most exquisite' and 'beautifully done'.[42]

William Theed also executed statues of Prince Albert for the Queen, the first of which was destined for Balmoral Castle, and appropriately shows him in Highland dress, with a deerhound by his side (Plate 10). The pose of this figure seems to derive from John Phillip's portrait of the Prince Consort commissioned in 1858 by Aberdeen Town Council (Plate 11), the oil sketch for which hangs at Balmoral Castle.[43] The Queen probably asked Theed to model his figure on this portrait because, as she told the Crown Princess, Phillip was 'our greatest painter', and 'darling Papa had such an admiration for him'.[44]

While staying at Osborne, Queen Victoria recorded in her journal on 1 January 1862 that she 'went down to see the sketch for a statue of my beloved Albert in Highland dress, which promises to be good'.[45] In May 1862 Theed travelled to Balmoral to discuss sites for the figure,[46] and the following August the full-size plaster model was despatched to the Castle to be tried in different positions. (The time and difficulty involved in transporting the cast from London and back emphasises the Queen's determination that the statue for their Highland home should be absolutely right.) Eventually a place at the foot of the staircase was decided upon, and when, after two hours' hard work, the cast was finally erected, Queen Victoria observed that it 'looked most beautiful & so life like'.[47] On 26 August (Prince Albert's birthday), the royal children 'placed wreaths of heather on the beloved & beautiful statue'.[48] The cast remained at Balmoral until the Queen returned to London when it was dispatched to Theed's studio for execution in marble.[49] The completed statue—'a wonderful likeness'[50]—was unveiled at Balmoral at a ceremony attended by the Queen, members of the royal family and household on 17 October 1863.[51] The inscription

10. William Theed: *Prince Albert in Highland dress*, Balmoral, from *The Illustrated London News*, 27 August 1864.

12. G.H. Thomas; *Unveiling of the statue of Prince Albert at Balmoral*, Royal Collection.

on the pedestal—'His life sprang from a deep inner sympathy with God's Will, and therefore with all that is true, and beautiful, and right'—was a phrase used by Norman Macleod in a letter to the Queen, dated 28 December 1861, which she transcribed into her *Album Inconsolativum*.

Soon after the unveiling, Queen Victoria decided to present a bronze replica of the statue to the tenantry of Balmoral. In June 1864 a painted plaster cast was tried out on the chosen site in the Castle grounds,[52] but on inspecting this, the Queen decided that it was too small, and ordered a colossal statue instead which would be 'seen from everywhere'.[53] This was cast in bronze by the firm of Elkington's that autumn, erected on a base of roughly-hewn stone, and unveiled on 15 October 1867 (Plate 12).[54] At Balmoral the Queen also marked the spot where Prince Albert shot his last stag,[55] and, following Scottish tradition, erected a cairn to his memory. The inscription on this, selected by the Crown Princess, was taken from the Apocrypha, and for this reason was criticised in some quarters as 'playing into the hands of Rome'.[56]

Theed's most elaborate piece of memorial sculpture for the Queen was the life-size group showing Prince Albert and herself in Anglo-Saxon dress, which was also known as *The Parting* (Plate 13). The sculptor was working on the clay model when the Queen and Princess Alice visited his studio in March 1863 to 'superintend the head' of the statue of Prince Albert.[57] After another visit in March 1865, she noted that 'the beautiful touching group of us together' was far advanced in marble.[58] The completed work was unveiled in

13

11. (*facing page*) John Phillip; *Prince Albert in Highland dress*, Aberdeen.

a corridor in Windsor Castle on 20 May 1867.[59] In submitting his bill for the group (which had greatly exceeded his original estimate), Theed observed that the work had taken him five years to complete, the difficulties of the execution being exacerbated by 'the position of the figures, which rendered the necessary undercuttings, most laborious, but especially in the Statue of His Royal Highness'.[60]

The idea of depicting Prince Albert and Queen Victoria in Anglo-Saxon dress seems to have been suggested by the Crown Princess.[61] Subjects drawn from Anglo-Saxon history had been popular with artists since the 1760s, but the number of statues and paintings devoted to such themes reached a peak in the middle years of the nineteenth century.[62] Theed's group, while undoubtedly influenced by this artistic vogue, does not represent Prince Albert and Queen Victoria as particular characters from Anglo-Saxon history. Neither does it commemorate any entertainment at which they wore Anglo-Saxon costume: the royal couple had not chosen this period as the theme for any of the fancy-dress balls for which they showed enthusiasm.[63] Rather, the group symbolises the ties between the German and English peoples from their origin in the Anglo-Saxon period to the nineteenth century, and Prince Albert's marriage to Queen Victoria. The allusion would have had special meaning also for the Princess Victoria whose own union with the Crown Prince of Prussia had been conceived by the Prince Consort partly as a means of strengthening the bonds between England and Germany.

The group was given a Christian emphasis by the inscription, 'Allured to brighter worlds, and led the way', taken from Oliver Goldsmith's *The Deserted Village*. These lines occur in the description of the parson of the village of Auburn whose life was devoted to bringing himself and his flock nearer to God. Queen Victoria undoubtedly saw an analogy with Prince Albert whose 'pure, grand and great soul . . . always aimed at coming nearer to his Creator from his childhood'.[64] Goldsmith's poem closes with the death of the parson: like the Prince Consort, he too left behind a desolate wife and family.

The Crown Princess, who had conceived the idea for Theed's group, herself undertook the execution of a bust of her father with the assistance of the German sculptor Professor Hugo Hagen. She began modelling it in March 1863 in the hope that her mother would commission it in marble to give to her and her husband as a combined birthday and Christmas present.[65]

The Crown Princess based her bust on those by Marochetti and Theed, observing that 'though both are full of valuable truths; Marochetti's is the better work of art but the other is much more like'.[66] Towards the end of March 1863, the Crown Princess sent her mother photographs of the clay model.[67] Queen Victoria particularly admired the eyes, but preferred the mouth, chin and nose in Theed's bust: the latter feature she found 'too thick' in her daughter's work and she sketched corrections onto the photographs.[68] The Crown Princess vigorously asserted that it had been based on Theed's bust in all particulars except where she felt the sculptor to have erred: 'The nose is no thicker than Mr. Theed's it measures exactly the same in breadth, and the mouth is the very same as his with the only difference of the moustache being cut off straight instead of being a little turned in, wh. throws a different shadow on the lip of course . . . Theed's measurements have all been so carefully kept to except in the eyes wh. never pleased me on his, and the cheeks wh. seemed a trifle too round.'[69] Neither the Queen nor her daughter was entirely happy with the

15

13. (*facing page*) William Theed: *Queen Victoria and Prince Albert in Anglo-Saxon dress*, Royal Collection.

14. E.H. Corbould and William Theed: Christening gift from Queen Victoria to Prince Albert Victor, 1864, Royal Collection.

15. E.H. Corbould and William Theed: Christening gift from Queen Victoria to Prince Christian Victor, 1867, Collection of The Royal Green Jackets.

plaster model which was sent to England in the spring of 1864 for, in a letter of 6 May, the Crown Princess observed 'Perfect it is *not*, it *could* not be as it was not done from nature— I feel that the nose is not quite right, perhaps not delicate enough but as the general air and ensemble seemed good I was afraid of spoiling it by more alterations . . . You will want a little time to get accustomed to it—but I venture to hope you will like it more and more the longer you look at it. The carriage of the head has I think more Life in it than Mr. Theed's.'[70] The bust was executed in marble, not for the Crown Princess and her husband, however, but as a Christmas present from them to Queen Victoria in 1864.[71]

The Queen did, nevertheless, give sculptures of Prince Albert to members of her family. She sent a bronze bust by Marochetti to the Crown Princess for her son William in January 1862;[72] and the baptism of the Prince of Wales's son, Prince Albert Victor, on 10 March 1864 provided the occasion for her to commission a statuette for the new baby 'in Memory of Albert, his beloved Grandfather' (Plate 14). A second version (Plate 15) was presented by the Queen to another godson, Prince Christian Victor of Schleswig-Holstein, son of Princess Helena, for his christening on 21 May 1867.[73] The original was designed by E.H. Corbould, instructor in history painting to the royal family since 1851, and relates to a picture which he had just completed for the Queen (Plate 16). Both works take as their theme Prince Albert as a Christian Knight, and are inscribed with variations of the Biblical text from 2 Timothy Chapter 4, 'I have fought a good fight, I have finished my course, I have kept the faith.'

Corbould's painting shows the Prince Consort clad in medieval armour, and is based on Robert Thorburn's miniature executed in 1844 (Plate 17). This was the Queen's favourite portrait of her husband and after his death became so precious to her (perhaps because she observed that his features during his last illness bore an extraordinary likeness to it)[74] that she hardly let it out of her sight. It was only with the greatest reluctance, and on the condition that 'the glass was not removed', that she lent it to Theodore Martin to be copied for the frontispiece of the first volume of his biography of the Prince Consort.[75] Thorburn's painting was, however, a fancy dress piece, and Corbould transmuted this image into a pious one by making it the central panel of a *trompe l'œil* 'triptych', by surrounding it with Biblical scenes, and by depicting the Prince as a Christian Knight in the act of sheathing his sword, his good fight fought. The painting was completed early in 1864,[76] and almost immediately Corbould was engaged to design the christening present for Prince Albert Victor.

The statuette of the Prince Consort is a re-working of the figure in Corbould's picture, but it was modelled by Theed who copied the head from his own bust of Prince Albert.[77] The pedestal is decorated with figures representing Faith, Hope and Charity, also modelled by Theed; with verses composed by Mrs. Prothero, wife of the rector of Whippingham; and with coats of arms, roses, lilies and other enrichments in enamel. The imagery and verses of the front panel—including a white lily bent over a broken rose with the inscription 'Frogmore'—record Queen Victoria's great loss, and her joy at the birth of her grandson. The other two panels contain verses exhorting the newborn prince to emulate the virtues and exemplary life of the illustrious grandfather whom he never saw, so that he too might earn the rewards of heaven—symbolised by the ebony band set with silver stars around the base.[78] The christening present, which Queen Victoria described as *'most beautiful'*,[79] was given to Prince Albert Victor at Christmas 1865: the theme was to be taken up again by Henri de Triqueti in the effigy of the Prince Consort in the Albert Memorial Chapel (Plate 31).[80]

The Queen also gave statuettes and busts of Prince Albert to faithful servants. Dr. James

16. E.H. Corbould: Memorial portrait of Prince Albert in armour, Royal Collection.

17. Robert Thorburn: *Prince Albert in armour*, Royal Collection.

Clark, who had attended the Prince during his last illness, General Charles Grey, who had been Prince Albert's private secretary from 1849 to 1861, and Sir Charles Phipps, the previous private secretary to the Prince, were all given marble busts by Theed.[81] Theodore Martin, who was entrusted in 1866 with the formidable task of writing Prince Albert's official biography (a work which when it was completed in 1880 filled five volumes) received a knighthood—and a bronze reduction of the recumbent effigy from the tomb in the Royal Mausoleum at Frogmore.[82]

Queen Victoria was very concerned that a written record should be compiled to perpetuate the memory of her husband and their life together. In May 1863 she asked the Crown Princess to assist her by writing a description of a typical New Year's Day 'beginning with you children standing in our room waiting for us with drawings and wishes; Grandmama at breakfast, then you children performing something or a tableau, and your playing and reciting and in the evening generally a concert or performance with orchestra—then our wedding day the same ... and later my birthday perhaps ... and put down any picture of darling Papa's manner'.[83] These observations were intended by the Queen for a book which her children and grandchildren would inherit, and for General Grey's life of the Prince Consort which he was compiling under the Queen's direction. This latter work was also originally intended for private circulation among members of the family only, but for fear of a copy being 'surreptitiously obtained and published, possibly in a garbled form', it was decided to make the work publicly available.[84] Other commitments prevented Grey from undertaking a complete biography, and his account, *The Early Years of His Royal Highness the Prince Consort*, which was published in 1867, covers Prince Albert's life up to the first year of his marriage.

Queen Victoria's own *Leaves from the Journal of Our Life in the Highlands, from 1848 to 1861* was likewise originally intended for private circulation among her family and friends, but in order to forestall 'incorrect representations of its contents' appearing in the press, this volume was also published, in 1868.[85] Illustrated with Queen Victoria's own sketches, 20,000 copies were sold immediately, and the work quickly went into several editions.

The only literary work which Queen Victoria commissioned for publication immediately after her husband's death was a volume of his speeches and addresses, compiled by Sir Arthur Helps who later assisted her with *Leaves from the Journal*. This appeared in 1862 and was immediately translated into other languages. In writing the prefatory sketch of Prince Albert's character, Helps was directed by Queen Victoria, and he noted that some parts were rewritten 'six or seven times under the Queen's own supervision'.[86]

These early biographies of the Prince Consort by Martin, Helps and Grey, written at the Queen's command and under her close scrutiny, were intended to convey to the public the nature and extent of her loss, and perhaps reflect too keenly her view of her husband as 'an Ideal and a type of the heavenliest of Mortals'.[87] After his death, Prince Albert assumed the status of a saint in her eyes. She adopted capital letters for pronouns referring to him as a mark of pious respect; she described the placing of the body in the Royal Mausoleum as its 'translation';[88] and she kept anniversaries connected with his death and burial as 'holy days'.[89] A print after Thorburn's portrait of Prince Albert hanging over her grandson's cradle looked to her like that of 'a patron saint',[90] while in the upper part of E.H. Corbould's memorial 'triptych' (itself a devotional form), he is depicted exchanging his earthly crown for a halo. The casts of his hands and face, and locks of his hair were all treated as 'sacred' relics,[91] and the places which he had inhabited became hallowed ground to be marked with monuments or preserved as shrines.

Queen Victoria's worship of the Prince, her desire to preserve relics associated with him and their life together, and to fill her residences with his image, was an excessive manifestation of the nineteenth-century obsession with mourning. Although extravagant ritual displays of grief were customary at this date, these were generally of limited duration, and it was not frowned upon for a widowed partner to remarry quite shortly after his or her bereavement. There were early rumours that the Queen would 'get over her loss & *perhaps marry again*'[92]—but for her this would have been unthinkable. No one could replace Prince Albert for whom Queen Victoria's personal mourning never ceased, and for whom she ordered that official mourning should be 'for the longest term in modern times'.[93] The Queen was, as Lord Clarendon remarked, 'very watchful about what people do and how the mourning is observed. She sent back the other day all the papers she had to sign because the black margin was not sufficiently broad.'[94] She herself always used black-edged writing paper thereafter, and wore widow's weeds (and often her widow's cap—the 'sad cap' as Princess Beatrice called it) until the last days of her life. Although posthumous busts and paintings, and jewellery incorporating portraits of the deceased, were common features of Victorian mourning, the extent to which the Queen bedecked her person and crammed her residences with memorial images of her husband far exceeded normal nineteenth-century practice. Mourning became 'a sort of religion'[95] for her—and remained one. Queen Victoria's position, and her personal wealth, allowed her to indulge to the full her enthusiasm for mourning and monuments. This found its greatest expression in the Royal Mausoleum at Frogmore and the Albert Memorial Chapel, schemes so elaborate and costly that they deserve to be considered separately.

20

2. The Tomb and the Cenotaph

THE PRINCE CONSORT died prematurely and no positive arrangements had been made for his interment, although as early as 1843 he and the Queen had decided that they would eventually be buried together in a specially-built mausoleum (Plate 18).[1] Until this plan could be realised, however, Prince Albert's body had to lie in St. George's Chapel at Windsor, in close proximity to Queen Victoria's disreputable uncles—a prospect which filled her with the utmost dismay. The establishment of a new and separate Royal Mausoleum can be seen as a gesture by which Queen Victoria and Prince Albert sought to dissociate themselves from their Hanoverian predecessors, in much the same way as Louis-Philippe renounced his Bourbon ancestry by founding a mausoleum at Dreux in the 1830s for members of of the Orléans branch of the French royal family.

Mausoleum burial was, furthermore, becoming something of a tradition in the Saxe-Coburg family. Leopold of Saxe-Coburg-Saalfeld, later King of the Belgians (Queen Victoria's uncle), had remodelled a summer-house at Claremont, Surrey into a 'mausoleum' after the death of his wife, Princess Charlotte, although she was not actually buried there, but in St. George's Chapel, Windsor. A mausoleum was commissioned as a family burial place in Coburg after the death in 1844 of Prince Albert's father, Duke Ernest I of Saxe-Coburg. Queen Victoria's mother, the Duchess of Kent (Victoria of Saxe-Coburg), decided in March 1859 to build a mausoleum for herself at Frogmore in the Home Park at Windsor, which was to serve as a summer-house until her death.[2] It was in fact never used as such, being incomplete when she died in March 1861, and was still being built when, on 18 December that year, Queen Victoria, 'much upset', chose a site nearby for herself and Prince Albert.[3] Ludwig Grüner and Albert Jenkins Humbert, who had been selected by the Prince Consort to design the Duchess of Kent's mausoleum, were at once entrusted with the commission for the new one. Overall responsibility was given to Grüner, whilst Humbert was to take charge of purely architectural matters and to manage the execution of the scheme.

Grüner had been Prince Albert's most trusted artistic adviser. The Prince, while still a student, had met him in Rome where Grüner was working on a series of engravings after Raphael's frescoes in the Vatican. Prince Albert shared Grüner's enthusiasm and was encouraged by him to undertake the compilation of the Windsor Raphael corpus—an attempt to collect together, for the purposes of comparative study, photographic reproductions of all works attributed to Raphael. This pioneering art-historical exercise was completed after the Prince's death by his librarian Carl Ruland.[4] Grüner himself published studies of Renaissance ornament and was responsible for the Raphaelesque scheme of

18. Ludwig Grüner and A.J. Humbert: The Royal Mausoleum, Frogmore.

decoration in the Buckingham Palace ballroom built by James Pennethorne. A.J. Humbert had been introduced to the Prince by Thomas Cubitt, the builder of Osborne, and had proved himself as an architect in the remodelling of nearby Whippingham Church. Here the Queen was to employ him again in 1864, this time to design a monument (including a medallion portrait of Prince Albert by Theed) for the Royal pew (Plate 19).[5]

The Queen spent January 1862 at Osborne discussing plans for the mausoleum with Grüner and Humbert, who were constantly on hand with sketches, and she also corresponded

19. A.J. Humbert and William Theed: Monument to Prince Albert, St. Mildred's Church, Whippingham.

frequently with the Crown Princess who had seen Grüner in Berlin at the end of December and had herself put forward a number of ideas for the mausoleum.[6] Finally, with her Uncle Leopold's help, the Queen chose a Romanesque design, octagonal in plan, and similar to the Coburg mausoleum which had been built by Gustav Eberhard to a design sketched out by Prince Albert and his brother. Queen Victoria had described this as 'beautiful, and so cheerful' when she visited it in September 1860.[7] The decision pleased the Crown Princess, who believed that her mother was 'right in wishing it to be like the one at Coburg' and who expressed the hope that she might 'be allowed to contribute in some measure to beautifying it'.[8] In honour of Prince Albert's taste, Queen Victoria also decided that the interior should be decorated with paintings after some of the Raphael compositions which he had so admired. The sarcophagus was to be placed in the centre, and to carry a recumbent effigy of the Prince (and eventually one of the Queen as well).[9]

For fear of criticism, which would be painful for the Queen, it was decided that nothing should be published about the design 'till the Building is finished. *Then* there may be no objection.'[10] Despite all precautions, descriptions appeared in July 1862 in *The Morning Star* and *The Times*, and the latter, as Humbert told Phipps, 'had evidently been written by someone who had a good knowledge of the structure'.[11] Eventually the pressure from the newspapers for information could no longer be resisted, and in December 1862 as the structure approached completion, it was decided to allow *The Builder*—and no other paper—to publish a few details about the design, together with a plan and elevation.[12] Their account was submitted for royal approval in January and published on 28 February 1863.[13]

There was concern that the design would provoke public criticism for its Romanesque exterior (and even more for its proposed High Renaissance interior, so this was not yet published) amongst those who believed that Gothic was the only appropriate choice of style. Similar fears were expressed about the classical style of the Duchess of Kent's mausoleum. Bernard Bolingbroke Woodward, the Queen's librarian at Windsor, wondered if a public statement by William Tite, President of the Royal Institute of British Architects, might defuse any possible controversy, and he wrote to Colonel Biddulph on 12 January 1863, saying, 'You are most likely aware that the *Gothicists* are furious because of the choice of classical types for these two structures. And they would circulate any sort of caricatured misstatement about them—If there were a *plain and clear description* made public by a man in Mr. Tite's position, half this annoyance would be prevented.'[14] Nevertheless it seems to have been decided not to draw attention to the designs in this way.

Work proceeded on the mausoleum as rapidly as possible in the hope that the structure would be complete by the first anniversary of the Prince's death. On 27 January 1862 excavation of the ground began, and on 15 March the Queen, supported by her children, went 'with trembling steps' to lay the foundation stone.[15] About one hundred workmen were employed on the mausoleum through the firm of George Dines the builder and, once gas light had been installed, work on the site was able to continue late into the evening.[16] By the beginning of August the four main arches were completed in brick, a month later the level of the upper windows was reached (Plate 20), and in November, despite some bad weather and difficulties in obtaining materials, the dome was constructed. The Queen wrote to the Crown Princess at this time that 'the middle portion of the mausoleum will be quite ready (excepting the interior decoration) for the consecration and the day after, for what will be too dreadful for me to think of—and mention! But I have another great distress! viz: the granite sarcophagus will not be ready for some months, as various accidents occurred to the granite—but I have had a temporary one in stone made, which will be placed a little farther back, with a cast of the splendid, lying statue upon it, and the sacred, precious contents will only be moved from the one to the other, when the permanent one is placed there.'[17]

The sarcophagus had presented considerable problems. It was decided that it should be shaped from a single piece of Scottish granite, as the sarcophagus for the Duchess of Kent

20. The Royal Mausoleum, Frogmore, in building.

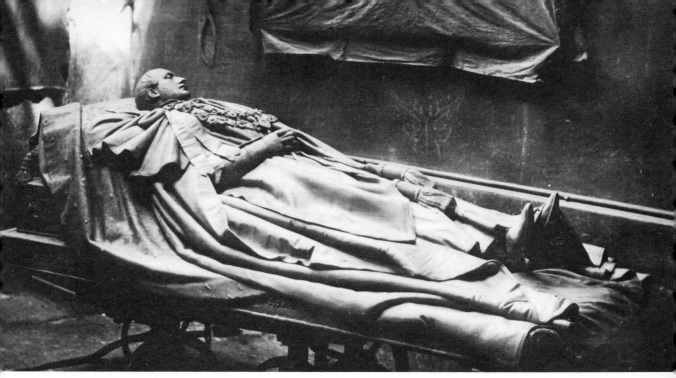

21. Effigy of Prince Albert in Marochetti's studio.

had been. But as it had to be big enough to contain two coffins, which required more space than most due to their incrustation of regal ornament, it was necessary to obtain a larger block of granite than had ever been quarried in Britain before.[18] Nevertheless the firm of Macdonald's of Aberdeen were willing to take on the task, but it took four attempts, and more than two years, before they succeeded in obtaining a large enough block.[19]

Baron Carlo Marochetti, a favourite sculptor of the royal couple, had been commissioned to carry out the Prince Consort's effigy almost as soon as the Queen had been able to collect her thoughts after her husband's death.[20] Whilst working on it, he had frequently turned to the Crown Princess for advice, not only in practical matters such as arrangements for the loan of the Prince's robes and uniform,[21] but also for the basis of the design itself. The Queen proudly recorded in her diary that 'Vicky had seen Baron Marochetti who had at once adopted her beautiful design for her beloved Father's statue' (Plate 21).[22]

Although Marochetti had managed to complete a plaster model of the effigy and everything seemed prepared for the anniversary of the Prince's death, the Queen still fretted continually, writing to Princess Alice on 24 November 1862, 'I feel *still* terribly anxious that *all* should be right for that *sad*, solemn event—wh. every day brings nearer. Every thing *should* be *ready beforehand*, so that the *day* AFTER the solemnisation, the "translation" wl. take place; & *all* be placed & closed.'[23]

The day of the consecration was wet, but such an occurrence had been anticipated and the Queen entered the mausoleum under a temporary covered way which was 'lined by the Choir of St. George's in their white surplices' to listen to the 'impressive ... but ... very affecting' service led by Samuel Wilberforce, Bishop of Oxford.[24] That night the Queen 'woke very often ... thinking of the sacred work to be carried out at 7 o'clock. At that hour the precious earthly Remains were to be carried with all love and peace to their final resting place' (Plate 22). At length when the task had been accomplished the Queen

25

22. Removal of the Prince Consort's remains to the Mausoleum at Frogmore, from *The Illustrated Times*, 27 December 1862.

23. The temporary sarcophagus and 'inner chapel' in the Royal Mausoleum.

went back to the mausoleum with her children and some of her Household, where 'the Dean [of Windsor], with a faltering voice, read some most appropriate Prayers. We were all much overcome, when we knelt round the beloved tomb. When everybody had gone out, we returned again & gazed on the great beauty & peace of the beautiful statue. What a comfort it will be to have that near me!'[25]

Once the Prince Consort's coffin was installed the question of its security became paramount. The desecration of the royal tombs at St. Denis in the wake of the French Revolution was too recent for anyone to be unaware of the potential propaganda value of a royal corpse or even a strategically placed piece of graffiti. The temporary sarcophagus was immediately enclosed in a carved wooden canopy or 'inner chapel' stoutly reinforced with iron (Sir Charles Phipps's idea)[26] which also protected the tomb from dust and dirt as building work continued (Plate 23). The Queen, who visited the mausoleum on 19 December 1862 as soon as the enclosure was completed, described how 'the gas light shone softly on the beloved features, as we gazed on them', and commented that 'the whole looks like some ancient shrine'.[27] The temporary sarcophagus in its protective 'chapel' is recorded in a photograph coloured by E.H. Corbould and mounted in a Gothic ormolu frame in the form of a triptych surmounted by a cross (Plate 2). Arrangements were made for the police to keep watch over the mausoleum,[28] but even before the end of the month a considerable scare was caused by the unauthorised entry of the local postman 'on the day Her Majesty gave permission for the servants to be admitted'.[29]

Although the structure of the mausoleum was more or less complete by the end of 1862, its decoration was barely begun and the rapid progress of work was not maintained. It was always understood that the cost was bound to be high, but Grüner was notoriously vague about financial matters and the actual costs consistently exceeded his estimates. At first, the Privy Purse Office were prepared to excuse him on account of his 'genius'. On 9 January 1864 H.T. Harrison wrote to Phipps that 'Mr. Grüner is too clever to be a good man of business, and does not readily comply with commonly necessary forms',[30] but two years later he considered him merely as 'a most troublesome person from his informal manner of

26

transacting business'.[31] Owing to the high costs it was decided that work on the interior would have to proceed more slowly than had originally been hoped.[32]

By November 1864 the granite sarcophagus was ready to leave Aberdeen. The Queen did not want it to be placed in the mausoleum until the decoration was further advanced, and suggested that it should be taken to Marochetti's studio. Macdonald's pointed out, however, that it should not be exposed to the risk of damage by more cartage than was absolutely necessary. As Marochetti required to refer to the sarcophagus when making the effigies and the figures of kneeling angels at the four corners, it was decided to store it in one of the transepts of the mausoleum.[33] On 28 November 1864 the Queen recorded in her diary that she 'saw from the window, while we were at breakfast, the sarcophagus going on a cart up the Long Walk.'[34] Two days later she 'Took a short late drive, stopping at the Mausoleum, on the way back. Found the sarcophagus partially unpacked & could look into it. It gave me a strange feeling to contemplate what is to be *our* resting place. Oh! could I but be there soon!'[35]

Marochetti had not long completed the marble effigies and the four angels when he died suddenly, in 1867. The figures remained in his studio until the following year when, despite delays in the arrival of items from abroad and the cessation of work during Queen Victoria's frequent visits, the mausoleum was considered finished enough for the removal of the

24. H.W. Brewer: *Visit of Queen Victoria to the Royal Mausoleum*, Royal Collection.

wooden canopy and the setting up of the permanent sarcophagus and the placing of the coffin within it (Plate 24). On 26 November 1868 the Queen was able to record that 'the sarcophagus has been closed & shut down—never to be opened but for me!'[36] Sculpture, paintings and decorative bronze work continued to arrive however until August 1871.

The mausoleum is entered through a porch lined with mosaic by Salviati and surmounted by a terracotta head of Christ, made by the Crown Princess and given by her to her father during his lifetime.[37] Inside, the decoration is High Renaissance in style, most of it in direct imitation of Raphael. Some of the artists who had worked on the interior of the Buckingham Palace ballroom were also employed here, notably the Italian painter Nicola Consoni, and also the firm of Barbedienne of Paris. It was generally felt that no British foundry was capable of such high quality cast work of Renaissance design at this date, and Barbedienne undertook the lamps and bronze enrichments for the mausoleum as well as the four bronze angels around the sarcophagus.

Consoni's work, copied largely from compositions by Raphael in the Chigi Chapels, dominates the interior. Above the entrance is a painting of the Cardinal Virtues with SS. Peter and Paul to either side. The schemes of decoration in the other three 'chapels' are based on the themes of the Nativity, the Crucifixion and the Resurrection.[38] Consoni was responsible for most of these paintings, but some were carried out by the German artists Frankl and Pfaender. Consoni also composed and painted the four Evangelists in the spandrels between the main arches, and designed the bas-reliefs of biblical scenes which were modelled by Hermann Hultzsch and cast in Dresden. The sculptors of the marble figures of prophets, which stand in niches beneath the Evangelist paintings, were selected as a result of a competition arranged by Grüner to find 'that artist or artists who comes nearest to the spirit of Raphael's Prophets',[39] but as they all came from Dresden, where Grüner was Professor of Fine Art, the contest must have been of a limited nature. Only two of the prophets—*Daniel* by Gustav Kuntz and *Solomon* by Friedrich Rentsch—were original designs, the other two—*David* by Heinrich Bäumer and *Isaiah* by Hultzsch—being based on figures in Raphael's fresco at Sta. Maria della Pace in Rome.[40]

Designs by Raphael were imitated wherever possible in the interior of the mausoleum— even if this meant, on occasion, changing the proposed subject-matter of the decoration. The Queen had at first wanted the Wise and Foolish Virgins to be painted over the entrance but no Raphael prototype for this could be found, and so the Cardinal Virtues from the Stanza della Segnatura in the Vatican were copied there instead. This approach to the decoration, with Prince Albert's Raphael corpus always in mind, imparts a pedantic character to the scheme.

Despite the pervasive High Renaissance flavour of the interior, a number of features from the inside of the Coburg mausoleum do also find a parallel here, in particular the strong outlining of the surfaces and the floor, inlaid with many coloured marbles in a bold geometric pattern, which had been noted by Queen Victoria on her visit to Coburg. The other item which had caught her eye on that occasion, and which is repeated here, is the 'marble altar' (Plate 25).[41]

At Frogmore, the marble altar was a somewhat contentious item. The Lutheran Church in Germany tolerated ecclesiastical features which were considered Popish in Britain. In 1845, Queen Victoria thought it worth recording that there was a crucifix on the altar of

25. The altar, Royal Mausoleum.

the chapel at Schloss Ehrenburg in Coburg, but noted that it seemed 'right' to her.[42] The expediency of having a chapel attached to the mausoleum at Frogmore had been discussed in January 1862 when the design was being drawn up: the Dean of Windsor voiced his opinion that if the mausoleum were to be the resting-place of Prince Albert and Queen Victoria only and were not intended for other members of their family, then it would not be worthwhile building a chapel alongside. He pointed out that a 'connexion with St. George'[s] might be maintained by commencing the service there ... and proceed[ing] thence at the proper period ... when all funerals pass out of the Church into the Church Yard'.[43] The Queen however was glad to sever the links with St. George's and its association with her predecessors, and it soon became apparent that she wanted more than the funeral service to be read at the mausoleum. To the Dean's embarrassment, she intended him to conduct a yearly memorial service at the tomb and also wished to use the mausoleum for her own private devotions. She required a proper altar. The Dean admitted to Lady Augusta Bruce that 'it is very true that in the course of the unhappy disputes that have arisen among parties in the church, that the fixed altar has been disallowed, in Law Courts, in Parochial Churches and Chapels', but he nevertheless 'told Mr. Humbert ... that I saw no objection to the table in the Mausoleum being a fixture', justifying his decision by an uneasy argument based on a difference of quality between the consecration of a mausoleum and that of a chapel.[44]

Grüner designed an altar which was to be enriched with 'mosaic work, lapis lazuli, bronze mouldings and rosettes' and a bas-relief after Raphael's *Deposition*. As usual he had to report that the costs would prove higher than he had anticipated, which provoked a tart reply from the Queen who was 'decidedly of opinion that the altar must not be allowed to be so expensive, and that the inlaying of the lapis lazuli is not at all necessary. Mr. Grüner must be kept within bounds. No one knew this better than the dear Prince'.[45] A simpler version of Grüner's design was therefore erected, without the lapis lazuli.

For those who sought such things, enough hints of Popery were apparent in the mausoleum for it to become a source of malicious rumour and outrageous conjecture. Little was known of it at first hand, partly because little had been the work of British artists. It was whispered that:

> ... eight thousand pounds of British gold
> The Queen did freely give to decorate

> Within, to one who came from Italy,—
> As if no British hand could trace such work[46]

The Altar, the ever-burning lamps, the 'special blue Police of Class A1 from Scotland Yard', and above all the heating system (normally considered unnecessary in a mausoleum) led to speculation that:

> a living priest—Mass Priest 'tis said
> A dark, a very dark designing Priest—
> A Jesuit Priest from Italy

was concealed therein, and that:

> ... Romish obyt thus is once more sung
> O'er his lone grave, or *Mass-oleum* called[47]

Queen Victoria and Prince Albert's decision to break with the tradition of royal burial in St. George's Chapel, Windsor also provoked an adverse reaction, and of a more widespread nature. Lord Clarendon is reported to have criticised the royal family's determination 'to set up insignificant tombs in that morass at Frogmore which is constantly flooded'.[48] The Dean of Windsor, who not unnaturally wished St. George's to retain its former importance as the royal burial place, and who believed that 'the principal objections of the Queen and prince were to the Vault of George 3rd underneath', had at first cherished the hope that the couple might be buried in the original Lady Chapel at St. George's, built by Henry VII for his own tomb but subsequently given by Henry VIII to Cardinal Wolsey. He pointed out that 'the nation also would ... be more more pleased with this arrangement than with the idea of the Queen and Prince being buried at Frogmore, a place of no celebrity, while the appropriation of so magnificent a shell as Wolsey Chapel for their sarcophagus, would be regarded with general satisfaction'.[49]

The Dean's proposal was rejected by the Queen who was intent upon realising her own and the Prince Consort's wish for a separate mausoleum, but she responded enthusiastically to the Crown Princess's suggestion that the Wolsey Chapel should be remodelled into an Albert memorial as a place of pilgrimage for the public (Plate 26).

At the Crown Princess's request, the Dean submitted her idea early in February 1862 to the architect George Gilbert Scott, who was engaged at this time in designing a window to the memory of Prince Albert for the east end of St. George's Chapel.[50] Scott was 'much struck and delighted' with the proposal, adding, however, 'that large funds (thousands) would be required to carry it out'.[51]

Financing the project was a difficult problem. The Queen suggested at first that the funds raised for the memorial window in St. George's Chapel should be diverted towards this new scheme. The Dean, however, was quick to rebuff this request: just as the Chapter had respected Queen Victoria's desire that the Prince should be buried at Frogmore rather than in St. George's, so they hoped that she would honour their wish to have a separate memorial in their own chapel 'close to where *he* is now'.[52] The Dean saw an opportunity to revive his plan for making the Wolsey Chapel into the Royal Mausoleum by adding persuasive financial arguments: not only would St. George's be willing to contribute funds if the Prince were to be buried there, but he thought that 'any amount would be obtained from the public either through Parliament or by subscriptions'.[53] Still unwilling to entertain

30

26. Albert Memorial Chapel, Windsor Castle.

this proposal, the Queen decided to approach Parliament herself for a grant, estimating the cost of converting the chapel into a memorial at £15,000 spread over two years, and agreeing to the admission of the public 'under proper regulations'.[54]

This request for public funds misled the government into believing that Queen Victoria wished the Wolsey Chapel to become the National Memorial to the Prince Consort.[55] Sir Charles Phipps hastened to correct this misapprehension: £15,000 would be 'unworthy' of the country, and of the Prince, for the National Memorial which moreover, 'could hardly consist of the execution of certain works within the Queen's Palace'. Her principal objection was, however, to the interference in the design and execution of the work that would inevitably follow any vote of public funds. Nevertheless, the Queen then sought to pay for the conversion by including a sum for the purpose in the estimates for works at Windsor Castle over the next three or four years.[56] Unfortunately she discovered that the money for works at the Royal Palaces and Parks had already been voted for 1862, and Lord Palmerston advised waiting until the next year rather than seeking a supplementary payment.[57] As a result of these 'hitches, troubles & difficulties', Queen Victoria decided in May 1862 to pay for the work herself.[58] The conversion of the Wolsey Chapel according to G.G. Scott's plans (which the Crown Princess had shown to her mother on 29 March 1862),[59] was to be undertaken in stages, as and when funds became available. Inevitably

31

this meant that the work took longer than the anticipated three or four years: remodelling began in 1862 but was not finally completed until 1875. The original estimate of £15,000 was also greatly exceeded.

Between July 1862 and August 1863 Henry Poole and Son were employed to replace the plaster ceiling with a vaulted one in Bath stone; to build a new doorway in the west wall; and to remove the south porch and door, with a view to bringing the shell of the Chapel into such a state as to permit internal decoration.[60] On removing the old ceiling, however, it was discovered that several of the oak beams were rotten, and the roof had to be secured by a system of iron ties and cast iron shoes.[61]

Scott had initially proposed to the Queen that the spaces between the ribs of the ceiling should be painted with angels and heraldic devices. In the summer of 1862, however, the Crown Princess suggested a more novel treatment—that the roof should be decorated with the marble tarsia pictures developed by the French sculptor Baron Henri de Triqueti.[62]

Triqueti's work as a sculptor had been known to the royal family for some time. Queen Victoria and Prince Albert had seen his monument to the Duc d'Orléans and his Pietà in the Chapelle de St. Ferdinand, Neuilly, during their visit to France in 1855.[63] In 1852 they had purchased his ivory group of *Sappho and Cupid*, and in 1858 a marble statue of *Edward VI*. The Prince Consort was also recorded to have expressed interest in Triqueti's marble tarsia—a process which involved the inlaying of different coloured marbles according to the flat tints of the picture, and then cutting out and filling with mastic the fine linear details. It was perhaps the display of two experimental panels at the 1862 International Exhibition in London, rekindling memories of Prince Albert's favourable impression of Triqueti's process, which prompted the Crown Princess to suggest the adoption of this technique in the ceiling of the Wolsey Chapel.[64]

G.G. Scott, however, pronounced that the size of the marble slabs in Triqueti's work rendered the process unsuitable for the curved surfaces of the roof, and, casting aside his initial proposal for painted decoration, he now suggested that the ceiling should be executed in Antonio Salviati's newly developed glass mosaic, specimens of which he had seen at the 1862 Exhibition that summer.[65] Scott wrote to the Dean of Windsor on 12 September 1862 that although the cost of decorating the ceiling by this method would be more than twice as much as by painting, he could not refrain from suggesting its adoption because of 'its suitableness to this situation and the magnificent effect it would give to the Chapel ... No decoration has ever been introduced which has so striking & noble effect for arched ceilings nor can I think of anything so suitable to this particular case.'[66] Salviati, who inspected the Wolsey Chapel the following day, was reported to be 'in a state of extacy [*sic*]' at the prospect of the commission, declaring that the variety of light upon the work would be 'truly magnificent', and that the mosaic would be 'absolutely indestructible by decay'.[67] The ceiling of Wolsey Chapel was one of the earliest examples of the use of Salviati's glass mosaic in England,[68] and its success undoubtedly prompted Scott to employ the firm again in 1865 on the Albert Memorial in Kensington Gardens.

Salviati's estimate was approved by Queen Victoria in October 1862.[69] The designs for the ceiling were prepared by Clayton and Bell under Scott's supervision, and small-scale drawings were submitted to the Queen in May 1863.[70] The full-size drawings were then sent to Salviati's workshop in Venice for translation into mosaic. The tesserae were assembled upside down on paper in small panels which were then shipped back to Windsor, fixed in position, and the facing paper removed.[71] The ceiling was completed by June 1864.[72] The painting and gilding of the ribs of the vaulting were also executed by Clayton and Bell.

As the roof of the chapel approached completion, the question of the decoration of the walls, and the subjects for the stained glass windows were considered. The windows on the north and south walls depict the ancestors of Prince Albert, and were designed by Hermann Sahl, Queen Victoria's German librarian, and executed by Clayton and Bell. The windows at the east end depict scenes connected with the Crucifixion. It had been agreed that the lights of the window at the west end of the chapel (which were at that time blocked up) should be re-opened, and also filled with stained glass. The Crown Princess subsequently suggested to Scott that they should remain filled in, and the panels decorated with paintings continuing the series of portraits and armorial bearings in the windows on the north and south sides of the chapel.[73] In June 1864, having seen the completed ceiling, Scott changed his mind, and proposed to the Queen that the west window, and the panels on either side of the stained glass windows (which were to be decorated with armorials), should be executed by Salviati 'to obviate the otherwise isolated position of the mosaic work of the ceiling' and to ensure 'a unity of effect'.[74] Scott's estimate was approved, the Queen adding that she hoped 'this will be the last proposal for addl. outlay'.[75]

It had been decided in the spring of 1864 that Henri de Triqueti's marble tarsia pictures (which the Crown Princess had earlier proposed for the ceiling) should be substituted for the frescoes which Scott had initially planned for the decoration of the walls of the chapel.[76] When the Crown Princess learnt of the new scheme for the west window, she wrote indignantly to the Queen expressing her hope that the mosaic had not been definitely decided upon, 'as I fear it wd. quite spoil the effect of the rest. M. de Triqueti and I were of opinion that that part ought to be kept very quiet in tone—so as not to injure the effect of the rest of his work—I was thinking of a large composition wh. he wd. with his admirable taste adapt to the place.'[77] In reply, Scott stressed that mosaic work of '*tender* and *delicate* tones of colour and a quiet treatment' would be used to harmonise with Triqueti's work, and stated his opinion that 'the enamel mosaic will accord better with the stained glass of the open windows, than the incised marble of Baron Triquiti [*sic*] while its gold grounds would continue the idea of the work of the ceiling'.[78] The mosaics of the west wall include portraits of English kings and queens and ecclesiastics associated with the Wolsey Chapel, and heraldic devices.

Although his marble tarsia had been rejected by Scott for both the ceiling and the west window, Henri de Triqueti was engaged to execute a scheme of decoration for the walls of the chapel beneath the windows. He had submitted his proposal in May 1864, estimating that the work would take between seven and eight years to complete.[79] Triqueti's programme involved a series of marble tarsia pictures and bas-reliefs on the south and west walls of the chapel depicting stories from the Old Testament which demonstrate conspicuous virtues attributed to the Prince Consort such as steadfastness, duty, purity, prudence, justice and so forth. The tarsia pictures and bas-reliefs on the north wall allude to the acts of the Prince Consort by means of scenes from the Old Testament: *Solomon receiving the gifts of Kings* (Plate 27), for example, is intended to represent Albert's interest in the progress of the

And all the kings of the earth sought the presence of Solomon and they brought every man his present vessels of silver and vessels of gold.

27. (*left*) Henri de Triqueti: *Solomon receiving the gifts of Kings*, Albert Memorial Chapel.

28. Susan Durant: *Prince Leopold*, Albert Memorial Chapel.

arts and manufactures, and his promotion of international exhibitions for their encouragement. The tarsia pictures in the east end of the chapel are devoted to the Passion of Christ.

The tarsia pictures were executed by Triqueti's former pupil, Jules C. Destréez. They were considered to be an improvement on the Baron's original experiment, particularly for the greater use of different coloured mastics, in addition to black, in the incised lines.[80] Destréez had also developed a new technique which not only improved the adherence between the mastic and the marble, but also permitted the reproduction of the finest details of Triqueti's drawings.[81] Twenty-eight different marbles from Great Britain, France, Italy, Greece and Belgium were used for the pictures,[82] while the surrounding borders were executed in Florentine mosaic—an inlay of semi-precious hard stones.

Above the tarsia pictures and bas-reliefs on the north, south and west walls, Triqueti placed medallion portraits of Queen Victoria and Prince Albert's nine children and the Princess of Wales,[83] the execution of which was entrusted to Susan Durant, Triqueti's favourite pupil. She began her work in the winter of 1864, and during the next three years she stayed regularly at Windsor and Osborne, modelling the portraits of the royal children.[84] Queen Victoria took great personal interest in the medallions, recommending, for example, that the eye in the relief of Princess Alice should be placed lower, and suggesting that Prince Leopold should be shown looking upwards, on account of his weak chin (Plate 28).[85]

In March 1868, Susan Durant accompanied the Queen to the chapel to inspect Triqueti's tarsia work, the first panels of which had arrived from his Paris studio the preceding winter.[86] She reported that 'the beauty of the marbles was quite a surprise to her [the Queen]. She said that much as she had heard of them she had no idea of anything so beautiful!' She added to her confidante, 'I must keep for your private ear what H.M. said of Mr. Scott, & how *she* trusted the direction of Mr. de Triqueti's part of the work would not be interfered in ... by H.M.'s special command, Mr. de T. is to meet Scott at the

34

Deanery where will be communicated the royal wish that the architect will adapt himself to the requirements of the artists!'[87] Durant here alludes to the deteriorating relationship between the architect and Triqueti, now a firm favourite of the royal family, and whose part in the completion of the chapel threatened to overshadow Scott's role as designer of the whole scheme.

Scott regretted the introduction of Triqueti's marble tarsia work which he did not consider 'worthy of his fame or its object'.[88] He also resented the sculptor's deviation from his design for the Florentine mosaic borders of the pictures, observing that 'For this I gave full drawings which have been entirely ignored, and I feel bound to say that the foliage substituted is by no means to my taste.'[89] The execution of the marble benches beneath the tarsia pictures, and the reredos at the east end were also entrusted to Triqueti—to Scott's regret. The architect commented later that he 'was sorry to observe that Baron Triqueti had deviated in some degree from my design for the seats as he before had done in respect of the inlaid foliage ... as his knowledge of Gothic architecture is very limited, I am anxious that such should not be the case in respect of the Reredos or other remaining parts'.[90] Triqueti evidently wished to design the entire reredos himself, but the Dean of Windsor prevailed upon the Queen to retain Scott's original scheme for the surround.[91] The reredos is, as a result, obviously the work of two hands, for Triqueti's bas-relief of the Resurrection rests uneasily in the frame designed by Scott. It was completed in December 1873.[92]

Triqueti not only asserted his artistic independence in works entrusted to him, but also interfered in matters that should have been Scott's exclusive domain. The architect felt that, for the harmony of the whole scheme, the window frames and other parts of the chapel should be painted. Queen Victoria expressed reservations about the extent of the colouring when Scott submitted his design in May 1872, and suggested that a small part should be carried out by which to judge the effect.[93] Clayton and Bell duly coloured a portion of the stonework of the windows in an endeavour to link the ceiling with the marble decoration of the walls, whereupon Triqueti composed a memorandum expressing his outrage at 'les insupportables essais de peinture récemment tentés au bas des fenêtres'. He asserted that colouring and gilding should be partial but, in accordance with medieval precedent, the stonework was entirely painted.[94]

Scott was also involved with the initial planning of the cenotaph of Prince Albert (Plates 29 and 30), the execution of which was entrusted to Triqueti in December 1865.[95] Queen Victoria had earlier instructed Scott that this should be carried out 'in a strictly medieval character' and should be based on Henry VII's tomb in Westminster Abbey (oddly, since this must have been recognised as among the earliest examples of Renaissance design in England). The recumbent effigy of the Prince Consort was to be dressed

in the robes of the Order of the Garter but not the *modern* ones but the cloak wh. was covered all over with the devices of the Order ... the feet of the figure shd. be supported by a Lion and Unicorn with the Arms, and the Pillow on wh. the head of the figure rests might be supported by 2 small kneeling figures of Angels. The Pces. Coronet and a helmet with his Crest should appear—also a sword. The chain of the Order of the Garter shd. be round the neck as worn at those times.

29. Henri de Triqueti: Cenotaph of the Prince Consort, Albert Memorial Chapel.

30. Henri de Triqueti: Effigy of the Prince Consort, Albert Memorial Chapel.

All devices and badges seen might be gilt and even in some places enamelled.

Round the pedestal there ought to be niches for small figures—(such as on Queen Elinor's tomb)—wh. figures might represent the members of the Pces. family. Such as his Parents his brother his children &c . . .—with the arms and mottoes & names of each. The whole should be in bronze with the details gilt and enamelled at pleasure.[96]

When the commission was given to Triqueti in 1865, however, the Crown Princess, presumably with the Queen's concurrence, instructed the sculptor to represent the Prince Consort in medieval armour 'enrichie avec le plus grand soin d'ornements éxecutés en damasquines d'or et d'argent, de manière à égaler, s'il était possible, les plus beaux travaux connues du 15me Siècle'.[97]

Medieval recumbent effigies began to be seriously imitated from the 1840s, and by the 1860s the vogue was well established.[98] None of the earlier examples depict the figure in medieval dress, however, and many critics were opposed to the historical incongruity this would imply. Even the arch-Gothicist A.W.N. Pugin admitted that 'to represent persons of the present century in the costume of the fourteenth, is little less inconsistent than to envelop them in the Roman toga'.[99] The decision to depict Prince Albert in medieval armour therefore marks a new treatment for nineteenth-century English sculpture, and was perhaps prompted by the recent completion of Corbould's triptych (Plate 16) and christening gift for Prince Albert Victor (Plate 14).

Triqueti initially professed consternation at the apparent anachronism of depicting a contemporary figure in medieval armour, and especially one whose triumphs had been in the field of peaceful, rather than of martial, arts. The sculptor resolved the dilemma in the same manner as Corbould, by taking as his theme the text 'I have fought the good fight, I have finished my course'. The armour was thus intended to symbolise the 'grand combat de la vie, et serait une allégorie Chrétienne aussi belle aussi poétique, que juste, que digne du Prince Consort'.[100] In consultation with the Crown Princess, Triqueti essayed different poses for the figure. In one early drawing the Prince Consort is depicted resting on his side (Plate 31),[101] while in a terracotta sketch model dated 1871 (Plate 32), he is represented fully recumbent in an attitude of prayer, with a dog (symbol of fidelity) at his feet replacing the lion and unicorn suggested by the Queen.[102] Triqueti finally decided to show the Prince in the act of sheathing his sword, his good fight fought, as in Corbould's images.

The sculptor did not follow Queen Victoria's original idea for members of the Prince's family to be represented like medieval 'weepers' around the base. Instead, Triqueti at first proposed figures of kneeling angels at the corners in the act of lifting the effigy of the Prince heavenwards and, between them, recessed panels decorated with coats of arms. These heraldic devices were later changed to two angels and statuettes representing Truth, Justice, Charity, Hope, Mourning Science, and Mourning Royalty (Plate 33)—a crowned figure, presumably intended to represent Queen Victoria, kneeling on a prie-dieu emblazoned with the Royal Coat of Arms, in a niche beneath Prince Albert's feet. Changes were also made in the choice of materials. The effigy and statuettes were executed in marble instead of bronze, and the gilt and enamel originally proposed for details of the Prince's armour and decorations were abandoned.

Progress on the sarcophagus and on the remaining tableaux for the walls was interrupted

31. Henri de Triqueti: Sketch for the effigy of the Prince Consort, Royal Archives.

32. Henri de Triqueti: Model for the effigy of the Prince Consort, Musée Girodet, Montargis, France.

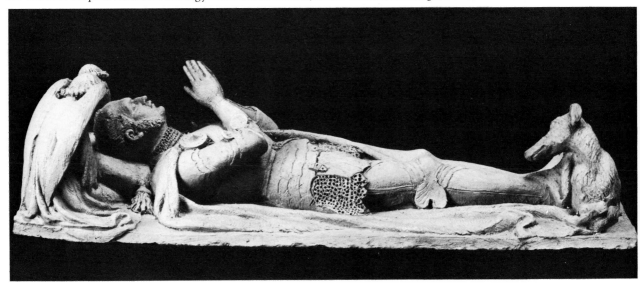

33. Henri de Triqueti: *Mourning Royalty* from the cenotaph of the Prince Consort, Albert Memorial Chapel.

by the Franco-Prussian War and by the siege of Paris. Triqueti remained in his studio in Paris for some time executing the work himself, his German and French assistants having left to join their respective armies. Eventually he was also forced to leave Paris, but not before burying the two remaining tarsia pictures and the sarcophagus (which was by then two-thirds complete) in deep trenches to avoid damage.[103] Triqueti was unable to regain access to his studio until early in the summer of 1871 when he reported that the works had sustained no injury.[104]

The base of the cenotaph was completed in 1871, and erected in the winter of 1872.[105] For the statue of Prince Albert, which he commenced in the summer of 1871,[106] the sculptor was lent by the Queen several plaster casts, including one of his favourite hound Eos.[107] The head of the Prince Consort was modelled from photographs and from the Crown Princess's bust of her father.[108] Triqueti arrived in England with the completed effigy in June 1873.[109] The Queen, who inspected it in the company of the sculptor on 4 July, pronounced it 'quite beautiful ... quite in the style of the old Monuments'.[110] Triqueti brought with him photographs of the models for the two angels which were intended for the niches on either side of the west door. The subjects of these—the Angel of Death and the Angel of Resurrection—had been determined by the Crown Princess,[111] but the sculptor did not live to see these, his last contribution to the chapel, executed in marble. Triqueti had been plagued with ill health for some time, and in May 1874 he died. Shortly afterwards, on 11 July, when Queen Victoria visited the chapel, she could not avoid commenting on the premature deaths of so many of the artists involved in executing memorials to her deceased husband: 'It is all but completed, & he [Triqueti], poor man, like Marochetti, and poor Miss Durant were not permitted to live to see their work finished. The reredos is put up & the 2 last statues have been completed in marble since his death[112] ... The marble floor is also laid down & very handsome. The Cenotaph is very beautiful & I saw it with poor Triquetti [sic] himself last year.'[113] The sculptor is reported to have expressed on his deathbed his regrets that he had been unable to show his completed work to the Queen, and also to have professed his great admiration for the Prince Consort, 'the greatest & best man he had ever known'.[114]

The chapel, which was renamed the Albert Memorial Chapel on completion, was opened to visitors for the first time on 1 December 1875. People were astonished by the richness of the interior which was described as 'a casket of gems',[115] and a 'veritable treasure-house of gilding, marble, mosaics, precious stones, and coloured glass'.[116] They were also impressed by the new techniques and materials so prominently displayed there.

In many ways the Albert Memorial Chapel presents a contrast with the Royal Mausoleum. It is far more imaginative in character, and incorporates original and experimental ideas in design and materials. The thoroughly 'medieval' effigy is at this date unique in England. The Chapel was intended by the Queen to be a place of pilgrimage for the public and this is emphasised by the use of the Gothic style which is associated with such royal shrines as Westminster Abbey and Gloucester Cathedral. The proliferation of sacred places associated with the remains of one individual was common in the medieval period. Eleanor of Castile, for example, was buried in Westminster Abbey, but her heart was preserved at the Church of the Friars Predicants in London, and the rest of her viscera were deposited in the Lady Chapel at Lincoln Cathedral. The Prince Consort was buried in one piece at Frogmore, but the idea of another 'tomb-chest' in the Albert Memorial Chapel recalls medieval practice. In this case, however, the true tomb was kept strictly private, whereas the cenotaph was a focus for the public tributes hoped for and encouraged by the Queen.

3. Shrines

THE NATIONAL MEMORIAL to His Royal Highness the Prince Consort (Plate 43), or *the Albert Memorial* as it has come to be called, needs little introduction—it is one of London's most familiar landmarks and the best-known monument of the Gothic revival.[1] For sculptors it was the most prestigious commission of the whole Victorian period, and presented an unparalleled opportunity to display their talents for large-scale statuary. For the architect, G.G. Scott, it was an exceptional chance 'to erect a kind of ciborium to protect a statue of the Prince ... designed in some degree on the principles of the ancient shrines. These shrines were models of imaginary buildings, such as had never in reality been erected, and my idea was to realise one of these imaginary structures with its precious materials, its inlaying, its enamels, etc. etc.' He went on to claim, somewhat inaccurately, that 'this was an idea so new, as to provoke much opposition'.[2] The technical problems presented by the lavish enrichments certainly did cause doubtful murmurings, but Scott's basic idea of a canopied structure enclosing a figure was not in itself original.

The form had been established in Britain twenty years earlier with George Meikle Kemp's monument to Sir Walter Scott, in Edinburgh (Plate 34), but in 1850 it fell abruptly from public favour after canopied monuments were used to commemorate the Protectionist politicians, Henry Handley and Lord George Bentinck.[3] The policies which these men stood for were still so topical and controversial at the time of their deaths (both men died young) that in the case of the Bentinck Memorial in Mansfield (Plate 35), the proposed statue eventually had to be omitted for fear of defacement. Thomas Chambers Hine's design for the canopy was, however, published in *The Builder*, which broadcast the implication that the 'protection' afforded by such monuments in some way represented the politics of Protection.[4] For ten years subsequently no memorials of this type were erected in Britain. It was not until 1861 that the form was revived in the monuments to the poet John Leyden in Denholm and to the Protestant martyr Bishop Hooper in Gloucester, which was unveiled the following year. These were not well-publicised schemes, however, and the most important precedent for Scott's design is another Albert Memorial—that put up in Manchester (Plate 36), the reputation of which has been somewhat eclipsed by its more ambitious successor.

On 6 January 1862 a meeting was held in Manchester Town Hall to discuss the erection of 'a fitting and enduring monument to the memory of the late lamented Prince Consort'.[5] Manchester was indebted to Prince Albert for his help with the planning of the Art Treasures Exhibition which had been held there in 1857, and the city's Albert Memorial represented another attempt to raise its cultural status. A committee (which included the

34. (*above left*) George Meikle Kemp:
Monument to Sir Walter Scott,
Edinburgh.

35. (*above right*) Thomas Chambers
Hine: Monument to Lord George
Bentinck, Mansfield, Nottinghamshire.

36. Thomas Worthington: Albert
Memorial, Manchester.

architect Thomas Worthington) was set up to collect funds and to determine the best way of using them. The subscription was opened by the mayor, Thomas Goadsby, who tried to influence the proceedings by stating that he was prepared to give £500 towards a statue or £100 if the memorial were to take some other form.[6]

Despite the mayor's proposal, it was tempting for the committee to consider schemes such as libraries, hospitals and charitable trusts which would benefit the city in a more practical way. This was strongly criticised by *The Builder*, with the rebuke that 'it is as to the fittest form which a monument to a truly noble and beloved prince ought to assume and not of any "want", great or small, of "the people of Manchester", that they ought to be considering; and we earnestly hope that, under the circumstances, they will cast aside all such mean, double-purposed, and selfish motives as that of their own wants'.[7]

In February 1862 the mayor offered to provide a complete statue in Carrara marble instead of simply a donation, so long as the committee were prepared to erect a suitable building for its 'reception and preservation'.[8] The committee accepted and the mayor commissioned a statue of the Prince Consort from Matthew Noble.[9] At this stage in the project, the 'receptacle' was considered basically as a protective measure for the figure, but the canopy which was chosen proved to be such an inventive and influential design that it quickly eclipsed in importance the conventional statue within.

Ideas submitted by the public had included several designs for canopies, and Thomas Worthington was also asked by other members of the committee to make suggestions as to the kind of structure in which the statue should be placed. He produced two alternative designs—one based on the Temple of the Winds at Athens, and the other, which the committee decided to adopt, was identical in all but a few details to the structure finally erected.[10] Queen Victoria expressed her approval, saying that nothing more beautiful or appropriate could be imagined,[11] but some commentators, notably the editor of *The Builder*, regretted the use of any historical style. He commented that 'placing the portrait statue of a man of our day beneath a Gothic canopy in the style of the fourteenth century, presents one of the most irreconcilable forms of incongruity to the eye of a thoughtful critic'.[12]

Work on the monument began in autumn 1863 but funds did not come in as quickly as had been hoped and the structure was not completed until December 1866,[13] although Noble's statue, showing Prince Albert dressed in Garter robes, had been ready for some time. To the great disappointment of all concerned (and especially, no doubt, Thomas Goadsby) no member of the royal family could be persuaded to attend the inauguration ceremony, which was held on 23 January 1867. The statue was unveiled by William Fairbairn, who was one of the most respected men in Manchester at this date.

The Manchester Albert Memorial carries a scheme of allegorical sculpture representing subjects in which Prince Albert showed interest—a scheme which was to be taken up again on the National Memorial. Each of the four pinnacles incorporates a free-standing statue with four small figures in niches below. These represent Art, supported by Music, Sculpture, Painting and Architecture; Science, supported by Astronomy, Mechanics, Chemistry and Geometry; Agriculture, supported by the Four Seasons; and Commerce, supported by Europe, Asia, Africa and America.[14] The spandrels of each main gable contain medallions with heads of eminent men 'representative of art and science', these being Michelangelo,

Wren, Inigo Jones, Raphael, Beethoven, Mendelssohn, Goethe, Schiller, Milton, Shakespeare, Tasso and Dante.[15] The great classical writers were all omitted in favour of Christians and another important criterion for selection seems to have been that the figures should have some personal relevance to the Prince Consort—a third of those chosen were Germans: Beethoven and Mendelssohn were amongst his favourite composers and, of course, his enthusiasm for Raphael was well-known. A *Schiller Anstalt* had recently been established in Manchester, which had a fairly large number of German inhabitants at this date—indeed, about one-twelfth of the subscribers to the city's Albert Memorial were German.

Although the Manchester Albert Memorial was by no means the earliest canopied statue, it was still unusual enough for James Prince Lee, Bishop of Manchester, to suggest to Worthington in 1863 that he should have a steel plate engraving published to establish his claim to be the first to design such a monument to the Prince Consort, as the competition for the National Albert Memorial was imminent. Worthington, however, did not think this worthwhile as 'a large number of photographs were in circulation' and his design had already been published in *The Builder* on 8 November 1862.[16] He was, perhaps, unwise.

On 14 January 1862, exactly one month after the death of the Prince Consort, a public meeting was held at the Mansion House in London, with the Lord Mayor, William Cubitt, in the chair. The meeting resolved that a memorial 'of a monumental and national character' should be erected to Prince Albert, and, it being evident that there was no other way to ensure unanimity, 'that the decision as to the nature and design of the proposed monument should be left to the Queen'.[17] A committee was appointed to set the scheme in motion. Subscriptions began to come in and the Queen was consulted immediately. Her reply, transmitted through General Grey, was clear:

> an obelisk, to be erected in Hyde Park on the site of the Great Exhibition of 1851, or on some spot immediately contiguous to it; nor would any proposal that can be made be more gratifying to the Queen personally, for she can never forget that the Prince himself had highly approved of the idea of a memorial of this character being raised on the same spot, in remembrance of that Exhibition.
>
> There would also be this advantage in a Monument of this nature—that several of the first artists might take part in its execution, for there would be room at the base of the obelisk for various fine groups of statuary, each of which might be entrusted to a different artist.[18]

She requested that a committee be set up to advise her, and the Earls of Derby and Clarendon, together with William Cubitt and Sir Charles Eastlake, President of the Royal Academy, were duly appointed.

The search began at once for a granite monolith for the desired obelisk. It was rumoured that a large enough piece might be quarried from the Duke of Argyll's land on the Isle of Mull, and the Ross of Mull Granite Company managed to excavate a single length of more than 115 feet, but this proved to be too narrow in the centre. Difficulties were also being encountered in obtaining a piece large enough for the royal sarcophagus and it soon became clear that the plan for a monolithic obelisk would have to be abandoned.[19] General Grey was concerned that the Queen had publicly expressed a hope which was to be disappointed, but she recorded that she 'felt relieved' when she heard the news.[20]

In the meantime, innumerable suggestions for various kinds of monument had been put forward by the public. Some of these were eccentric or impractical, but a growing body of opinion was in favour of combining the memorial with a 'work of utility'. This could not be ignored and when, in May 1862, seven distinguished architects were asked collectively to put forward ideas, they were required to bear this in mind and to consider a memorial 'in connection with an institution of arts and sciences' of the sort envisaged by the Prince Consort for South Kensington. Six of the architects selected—William Tite, Sydney Smirke, Philip Hardwick, M.D. Wyatt, T.L. Donaldson and James Pennethorne—worked mainly in classical styles. Only the seventh, Scott, represented the Goths. Not surprisingly, he expressed the view that each architect should be consulted individually,[21] but a single report was insisted upon and this was submitted on 5 June.

The seven architects recommended that the monument and the institution should be separate, because 'The Memorial, if erected in conjunction with any large building or institution, would lose in individual grandeur and importance; it would be difficult to treat it otherwise than as a subordinate object even outside the building; and if placed within, it would be seldom seen, and would not be the national monument immediately under the public eye, which most people are expecting.'[22] The site suggested for the memorial was the present one (with the institution to be where the Royal Albert Hall was eventually built), although the Kensington Road was to be straightened out to the south of it. This was obviously a suitable spot because 'It is at no great distance from the area occupied by the Exhibition Building of 1851, and is in immediate juxtaposition with the Horticultural Gardens (the result of the Royal Highness's own conception), thus forming a point of connection between the two.'[23]

The report's proposals as to the form the memorial might take were less precise. The Queen had given no guidance beyond insisting that a statue of Prince Albert should be prominent in any monument, and the architects' response was scarcely more defined. They suggested: '1st, an obelisk in several stones; 2ndly, a column; 3rdly, a Gothic Cross; 4thly, a large group or groups of sculpture, and 5thly, a building', each to be associated with a figure of the Prince. Various possible problems were mentioned, concerned mainly with the risk of any architectural structure swamping the statue, and with the question of the discolouration of bronze in the open air.

It is perhaps not surprising that no unanimous proposal was put forward. The architects may have been nursing hopes for their own ideas here and indeed the next step taken by the Queen's advisory committee was to approach each architect individually for a design. Tite and Smirke declined to compete and so Charles Barry and his brother, Edward Middleton Barry, were invited to submit plans in their place. The architects were each asked to produce designs, both for a monument and an 'institute', and to bear in mind the limit of the funds available—at that point, some £60,000.

The disadvantage encountered by Scott as a lone Goth in a group of classicists, turned to his advantage at this stage. His design must have caught the Queen's attention by virtue of its style alone when she considered the schemes early in February 1863. It was, in addition, beautifully presented and accompanied by a persuasive text emphasising the Prince Consort's approval of Gothic. The only rival to Scott's design in stylistic terms was an 'Italian Gothic Cross' put forward by Matthew Digby Wyatt, who also submitted plans for a

45

37. P.C. Hardwick: design for the Albert Memorial. Royal Institute of British Architects.

classical temple and for a sculptural group representing Fame crowning Prince Albert. All the other designs were classical—Pennethorne, Donaldson and the Barry brothers proposing 'buildings', with Charles Barry putting forward, as an alternative, an equestrian statue: 'The horse being in bronze, while the figure of the Prince himself is proposed of the new metal, aluminium, for the reason that its light grey tint and dead unburnished surface would, Mr. Barry thinks, be more fitting and effective than either bronze or gold for a *portrait* and for the display of the highest sculptural art.'[24] Hardwick submitted a plan for a colossal gilded bronze statue of Prince Albert on a pedestal carrying figures representing Peace, Art and Science, above a formal terraced garden with fountain pools and obelisks (Plate 37). This was the only scheme which could be carried out for the sum available—his estimate was £48,000.[25]

The Queen thought that only Hardwick's and Scott's designs 'would at all do' and she reserved judgement until she had consulted her eldest daughter who was due to arrive in England later in the month. The Crown Princess evidently preferred Scott's design (Plate 38) and the Queen's advisory committee concurred.[26] The only problem which remained was one of finance—Scott's estimate was at least £110,000 for the memorial alone. The scheme for the 'Hall of Science and Art' was therefore shelved—but extra funds were still needed. About £12,000 more was raised from the public and, on 23 April 1863, Parliament voted £50,000 towards the memorial. Scott's plan could then be realised.

Scott's accompanying text outlined the reasoning behind his design. He began, 'I have not hesitated to adopt in my design the style at once most congenial with my own feelings, and that of the most touching monuments ever erected in this country to a Royal Consort—the exquisite "Eleanor Crosses".'[27] The term 'Eleanor Cross' was often, at that time, used very loosely, to describe almost any free-standing Gothic monument,[28] but Scott's use of the expression here is somewhat misleading. The Albert Memorial is an open canopy enshrining a single statue, rather than a solid structure like the Eleanor Crosses, which incorporate several figures at a higher level, in niches—but Scott was well-known for designing that very type of monument. He had made his name in 1840 as a result of winning the competition for the Martyrs' Memorial in Oxford (Plate 39) with a design based on Waltham Cross (Plate 40), one of the three crosses surviving from the twelve put up by Edward I after Queen Eleanor's death in 1290.

The historical parallels between Prince Albert and the much-loved consort of Edward I

38. G.G. Scott: design for the Albert Memorial. Victoria and Albert Museum.

39. (*below left*) G.G. Scott: Martyrs' Memorial, Oxford.

40. (*below right*) Waltham Cross, Cheshunt, Hertfordshire.

had led some people to propose that an Eleanor Cross would be appropriate for the National Albert Memorial. *The Civil Engineer and Architect's Journal* had pointed out that this form was 'almost sacred to religious and marital memories' and suggested that 'Victoria of England might repeat upon the same site for Albert of Saxony what Edward of England did for Eleanor of Castile.'[29] The publication of Scott's text before an illustration of the design misled people into believing that an Eleanor Cross was to be erected. Whilst some commentators approved the choice for its suitability—one, for example, expressed the hope that 'future pilgrims will be found wending their way to the good Prince Albert's Cross'[30]—others were disappointed to discover that, when 'wanting an Albert Memorial', the country was to be 'forced to take an Eleanor Cross'.[31]

Scott continued the explanation of his design more accurately by pointing out that:

> The great purpose of an architectural structure, as a part of the Memorial, is to protect and overshadow the statue of the Prince. This idea is the key-note of my design, and my next leading idea has been to give to this overshadowing structure the character of a vast *shrine*, enriching it with all the arts by which the character of *preciousness* can be imparted to an architectural design, and by which it can be made to express the value attached to the object which it protects. The idea, then, which I have worked out may be described as a colossal statue of the Prince placed beneath a vast and magnificent shrine or tabernacle, and surrounded by works of sculpture illustrating those arts and sciences which he fostered, and the great undertakings which he originated.[32]

Not long after the selection of Scott's design, Captain Francis Fowke remarked upon its resemblance to the fourteenth-century shrine of the Madonna by Andrea Orcagna in the Or San Michele in Florence (Plate 41).[33] A much closer similarity seems however to have passed unnoticed. The National Albert Memorial follows the design of the thirteenth-century ciborium by Arnolfo di Cambio in the church of S. Paolo fuori le mura in Rome, not only in its general form but also in a number of telling details such as the niches containing small statues at the angles, the shape of the main arches and their cusping, and the use of figures in the spandrels (Plates 42 and 43). Scott admitted in his *Recollections* (which appeared in 1879, after his death) that 'the form is the same' as 'the ciboria which canopy the altars of the Roman Basilicas', but denied that it had been derived consciously[34]—a prudent assertion since the altar canopy had recently become a controversial issue. In 1873 the church of St. Barnabas, Pimlico, had been refused permission to erect a canopy (designed by Scott's former pupil George Edmund Street) over the altar, as the opposition convinced the Consistory Court that 'the real object of that application was to ... erect a monument of Popish superstition'.[35] The decision was widely publicised and generally approved, so it would not be surprising if Scott wanted to play down his dependence on such a structure in the formation of his Albert Memorial design.

Scott's only valid claim to originality lies not so much in his general idea of 'a kind of ciborium' but in his particular dependence on the design of a small-scale medieval example. By then it was generally agreed that 'an architectural canopy, as a protection and ornamental accessory to a statue is in itself a pleasing and appropriate device',[36] but no one had yet deliberately set out 'to translate back again into a real building, the idea which must

48

41. (*above left*) Andrea
Orcagna: Shrine of the
Madonna, Or San Michele,
Florence.

42. (*above right*) Arnolfo di
Cambio: Ciborium, S. Paolo
fuori le mura, Rome.

43. G.G. Scott: National
Albert Memorial,
Kensington Gardens.

have floated in the imagination of those ancient shrine-workers'.[37] Thomas Worthington for instance, knew and admired Orcagna's shrine in the Or San Michele, considering it 'a work of rare beauty, one which I could never forget' but his sources for the Manchester Albert Memorial are to be found in full-scale architecture.[38] Scott's sense of the flexibility of scale does, however, find a parallel in Ruskin, who could describe the cathedral of St. Mark in Venice as a 'jewelled casket' or 'a vast illuminated missal' and who described a missal as a 'fairy cathedral'.[39]

Not everyone shared this sense. Henry Cole, Director of the South Kensington Museum, and the most influential member of the original Mansion House Committee, believed that Scott's design was an absurdity in historical terms, and he was also worried about the practical problems of its realisation and maintenance. He compiled a *Memorandum on Crosses and Shrines in England* in which he pointed out that all surviving memorial crosses in this country rose as a solid structure from the base and that 'the Edinburgh Scott monument is the only example of a Gothic canopy surmounting a *sitting* figure in the *open air*, and has the affectation of affording protection to the figure, which it does not do. It was erected at an early period of the revival of Gothic architecture; it is an admitted failure and solecism, and is an example to avoid rather than to imitate.'[40] He went on to point out that open shrines of the kind upon which Scott's design was based were always placed within a building for protection. Scott's reply to these objections[41] convinced the Queen's advisers but Cole continued to voice his concern from time to time.

An executive committee, consisting of Grey, Phipps, Biddulph, Eastlake[42] and Sir Alexander Spearman (Controller General of the National Debt Office), was set up later in 1863 to arrange for the construction of the memorial. They at once accepted the offer made by John Kelk (at Cole's suggestion) for his firm to do the work at cost price—and himself to bear any excess over his estimate of £85,508. It was a wise decision, because Kelk's efficiency was exemplary. Work on the foundations begain in May 1864 and the construction was completed by June 1868, although the memorial was not opened to the public until 3 July 1872, because the sculpture was not yet complete.

The National Albert Memorial as erected differs little from Scott's design, the only important modifications being the heightening of the flèche—an alteration made under pressure from Henry Cole, and one which Scott later regretted[43]—and an increase in the number of shafts to the angle piers from four to eight, to give a greater appearance of strength.

A number of specialists were brought in to enliven and enrich Kelk's basic structure. The manufacturer of the flèche was F. A. Skidmore of Coventry, with whose contribution Scott was delighted, commenting that 'no nobler work in metal for architectural purposes has, so far as I know, been produced in our own, or probably—considering its scale and extent—in any other age; nor do I think that any man living but Mr. Skidmore could have produced such a work'.[44] William Brindley (of the firm of Farmer and Brindley) was responsible for the stone carving on the canopy, which was then gilded.[45] The upper parts were encrusted with glass mosaic and semi-precious stones, 'crystals, agates, cornelians, malachite, amethysts, porphyry of brilliant colours, and other objects of a similar kind'—which the public were invited to donate.[46]

Cole continued to insist that the decorative materials would not withstand exposure and

44. John Wills and Alfred Bedborough: design for a glasshouse to protect the Albert Memorial, Victoria and Albert Museum.

recommended that the whole monument be enclosed within a huge glasshouse for protection. This idea was taken up in 1876 by a Brompton gardener, John Wills, and a design was produced for him by Alfred Bedborough (Plate 44). Wills claimed that 'a suitable covering is absolutely necessary, not only to prevent a speedy disfigurement, through atmospheric influences, of the nation's memorial, but also to enable the admiring thousands . . . to enjoy, in all weathers, an inspection of the beautiful work of art'.[47] The proposal came to nothing but it is certainly singular that an architectural type which originated as a protective structure should here be the most vulnerable part of the memorial. Furthermore, this delicate canopy encloses a statue made of bronze, which is relatively robust, whilst the outlying groups of sculpture are of marble, albeit a particularly durable type.

Initially, it had been assumed that all the exposed statuary would be of gilded bronze, which it was hoped the government would provide, but, as Parliament had already granted £50,000 towards the memorial, they were reluctant to supply this also. Scott therefore selected for all the sculpture a marble which he believed would be capable of standing exposure—a type of Sicilian marble called *campanella*, which was not generally in much demand on account of its hardness. However, in autumn 1866 the government bronze became available and it was then decided that the statue of the Prince and the small figures at the angles of the canopy should be of gilded bronze, whilst the groups were still to be of *campanella*.

The sculptors for the figure of Prince Albert and for the allegorical groups were chosen by the Queen, but they were required to follow Scott's basic design, as set out in models by H.H. Armstead. For the Prince's statue Queen Victoria, as expected, selected Maro-

51

chetti, who was already working on his effigy for the Royal Mausoleum. The sculptor was, however, not content to work within the confines imposed by Scott. In the first place, Marochetti was unhappy that a figure seen from below should be shown seated, and would have preferred an equestrian figure, but Scott emphasised that his design 'absolutely required an enthroned effigy'.[48] Marochetti made two unsuccessful models and was working on a third at the time of his death in December 1867. The Queen hoped that his model could be completed by another sculptor but she was advised that it was not good enough— and a personal visit to the sculptor's studio in March 1868 confirmed this. No illustration of Marochetti's model survives, but, if it reflected his clumsy seated figure of the Prince at Aberdeen (Plate 79), it is easy to see why it was generally considered unsatisfactory.[49] Nevertheless, Marochetti's likeness of the Prince's face was thought good enough for the Queen to stipulate that Foley, to whom the commission was given in May 1868, should incorporate it into the new figure. Foley was already working on one of the sculptural groups for the memorial and was considered accomplished and professional in his approach. By December 1868 he had produced a model in which the squat effect of a seated figure was avoided by representing the Prince leaning forward 'as if taking an earnest and active interest in that which might be supposed to be passing around him'.[50] This pleased everybody and, although minor alterations were made, the full-size models simply consolidated this idea. The casting in bronze of the statue, by Henry Prince and Company of Southwark, was under way at the time of Foley's death in August 1874. The figure (Plate 45), which shows the Prince wearing the robes of the Garter and holding a catalogue of the Great Exhibition, was put in place in November 1875 and, after gilding, was uncovered in March 1876.[51] Oddly enough, there was no inauguration ceremony, perhaps because the structure had been complete and on view since 1872. The figure of Prince Albert presides over a scheme 'illustrating those arts and sciences which he fostered and the great undertakings which he originated'.[52] Most prominent amongst these are the eight sculptural groups.

The groups at the base of the canopy were put in place in the summer and autumn of 1870. They represent Agriculture, by William Calder Marshall; Manufactures, by Henry Weekes (Plate 46); Commerce, by Thomas Thornycroft; and Engineering, by John Lawlor—all skills which were 'furthered and promoted by the International Exhibitions ... which claim the Prince Consort as their great originator'.[53] The outlying groups, set up between autumn 1870 and summer 1872, represent Europe (Patrick Macdowell), Asia (J. H. Foley), Africa (William Theed) and America (John Bell). They are all technically highly accomplished but lacking in individuality. The sculptors were required to follow models made by H. H. Armstead to Scott's design, and they clearly felt constrained by this. Furthermore, once their own models were made, the Queen's advisers continually suggested alterations. The lifeless result reveals the dangers of design by committee. Scott himself admitted that he preferred Armstead's models to the finished works.[54] Only the figure of Asia unveiling herself (Plate 47) retains an appearance of spontaneity. The allegorical references are often laborious and obscure—the portrayal of Asia turns out to be 'an allusion to the important display of the products of Asia, which was made at the Great Exhibition of 1851', whilst the elephant upon which she sits 'is intended to typify the subjection of brute force to human intelligence'.[55] *The Saturday Review* remarked that

45. J.H. Foley: *Prince Albert*, National Albert Memorial.

46. (*below left*) Henry Weekes: *Manufactures*, National Albert Memorial.

47. (*below right*) J.H. Foley: *Asia*, National Albert Memorial.

48. Sculptors' studios around the National Albert Memorial.

Asia's action was more likely to suggest to the average spectator that the young lady was removing her dress for a dip in the Ganges.[56]

The figures of the frieze around the podium of the Albert Memorial are more dynamic than those in the groups above. Those on the south and east sides ('poets and musicians' and 'painters') were considered particularly successful—and it is interesting to note that Armstead was here responsible for both layout and execution. Unlike the sculptors of the groups, who were well-known and established, those who carved the frieze, Armstead and J.B. Philip (who was responsible for the 'architects' and 'sculptors') were comparative newcomers and, moreover, had worked chiefly in an architectural context. Scott, who appointed them, had been an admirer of Armstead's work for some time, and had engaged Philip to work on his reredos in St. George's Chapel, Windsor, but an additional consideration in his selection of these two may well have been that of cost. Younger sculptors, whose reputation had yet to be secured, were likely to be prepared to do the work more cheaply than established men—and there was some argument over the fees to be paid for the groups (during which Bell remarked that 'sixty years of age is rather late in the day to be paid by advertisement'!).[57]

The frieze was carved *in situ* ('hewn, or, more properly, *excavated* out of the solid mass of the monument')[58] and the sculptors' studios surrounded the memorial until spring 1872 (Plate 48). The theme of the frieze derives from Delaroche's *Hémicycle des Beaux-Arts* in the Ecole des Beaux-Arts in Paris—a source which the architect himself acknowledged.[59] Scott's arrangement 'avoids selecting either of the three commonly received fine arts (... Painting, Sculpture and Architecture) for the foremost place—but it places Painting and Sculpture on the two flanks united in front by Poetry as their *ideal* bond of union and by Architecture behind as their *material* bond of union'.[60] Great care was taken to achieve accurate portrait likenesses where such existed.[61] Scott was the only living person to be

54

49. J.B. Philip: *Architects*, National Albert Memorial.

50. John Clayton: *Sculptura*, National Albert Memorial.

included (he is behind Pugin in low relief, Plate 49)—and it is interesting that Arnolfo di Cambio is also included amongst the architects.[62]

In the gable of the canopy above each face of the podium is an enthroned personification (Plate 50) of the art whose most eminent professors (or those considered such in the 1860s) are sculptured beneath. These were designed by John Clayton (of Clayton and Bell) and executed in Venice by Salviati, who was already working on mosaics for Scott in the Albert Memorial Chapel at Windsor. Cole expressed concern over the durability of outdoor mosaic in the climate of northern Europe and, in autumn 1863, reported that the only exposed mosaic he had discovered north of the Alps—fourteenth-century work on Prague Cathedral—had seriously deteriorated.[63] Nevertheless, Salviati's work has weathered well, which is particularly fortunate because the inscription is also executed in glass mosaic. It reads: 'QUEEN VICTORIA AND HER PEOPLE · TO THE MEMORY OF ALBERT PRINCE CONSORT · AS A TRIBUTE OF THEIR GRATITUDE · FOR A LIFE DEVOTED TO THE PUBLIC GOOD.'

As the themes explored in the podium are 'idealised' at a higher level,[64] so the smaller allegorical figures in the body of the shrine become progressively more pious towards the cross at the summit. At the angles of the memorial, against the piers and in niches immediately above, are bronze statues by Armstead and Philip (cast by Elkington's) which represent the practical arts and sciences. The figures in the flèche above were executed by James Redfern, and were originally gilded. First is a rank of Christian and Moral Virtues and just below the cross are two tiers of angels, the lower portrayed in 'attitudes suggestive of the resignation of wordly honours' and the upper revealing 'aspiration after heavenly glory'.[65]

On the whole the National Albert Memorial received a favourable press, although it was criticised on several counts, notably its apparent top-heaviness and, paradoxically, its preciousness which was thought not to convey the sense of timelessness and immutability fundamental to monumental art. One reviewer described it as an 'architectural bravado' lacking in actual security and 'true monumental character'.[66] *The Pall Mall Gazette* observed 'instinct trembles, however calculations may reassure, for the personage to be enshrined beneath this vast mass resting on four such moderate supports'.[67] Neither was the richness a substitute for monumental grandeur. In 1863 *The Civil Engineer and Architect's Journal* criticised Scott for not producing 'something beyond lavish extravagance of ornament and costliness of material',[68] and another reviewer referred to the memorial as exhibiting 'beauty rather than bulk, richness rather than gigantic'.[69] *The Saturday Review* observed that 'the Albert memorial is beautiful in detail, but lays no claim to grandeur in the mass; it suffers by proximity to the Albert Hall; the memorial is dwarfed into an art toy by its neighbour, the gigantic gasometer of science and musical sound'.[70]

The gravest doubts expressed, however, were as to whether the National Memorial actually fulfilled its function of commemorating Prince Albert. *The Athenaeum* argued that the subjects of the allgorical groups and the podium reliefs were what the monument actually immortalised and therefore it far better commemorated the Great Exhibition of 1851 than Prince Albert as an individual.[71] *The Times* was more emphatic: 'We are struck with the extraordinary omission which has been made in introducing nowhere so much as a single word of inscription, or emblem of sculpture or ornament, which might declare to posterity the real *raison d'être* of the splendid shrine! Why was it that when Prince Albert

56

51. J.H. Chamberlain: Monument to George Dawson, Birmingham.

died the nation felt it had suffered a loss heavy and irreparable? Why is it that national sympathy and national money have raised this Memorial?' The writer concluded that it was not because Albert had promoted art and science but because 'all felt that so princely an example of purity of life could ill be spared by a wealthy and luxurious age and society'. Yet the memorial showed Albert 'seated eternally in bronze, surrounded by groups and statues of arts fine and useful, of sciences exact and vague, but with not a single figure, word, or emblem of all those which are below him, about him, and above him, to tell posterity what it really was that moved the English people so gloriously to enshrine his memory. The Memorial is beautiful, but it is quite idle to talk about its "motive", when from cross to stairs it is *Hamlet* with the part left out.'[72] The concept of the memorial was no longer in any doubt, however, and even *The Builder* went along with the general consensus that it was 'the finest modern work of its kind'.[73] Scott was given a knighthood as a result.

Both the Manchester and the National Albert Memorials strengthened the popularity of canopied statues. Other cities contemplated Albert Memorials of this form. The committee at Dublin wrote to that at Manchester asking to be sent a sketch of Worthington's design, as they had collected about the same amount of money as Manchester and were thinking about putting up a similar monument.[74] In Birmingham, Foley had been commissioned to execute a statue of the Prince in Carrara marble, and it was proposed to protect the figure with a Gothic canopy, designed by J.H. Chamberlain.[75] Apparently, owing to the failure to find a suitable site for the monument, the canopy project had to be abandoned and, to protect it from the atmosphere, the statue was placed in Birmingham Art Gallery.[76] Although Chamberlain's design for the canopy is now lost, his monument to George Dawson (Plate 51), erected in Birmingham in 1881 (and since demolished), reveals the extent to which he was influenced by Scott's scheme. Canopied monuments continued to be popular, but the vast scale and lavish decoration of the National Albert Memorial were never equalled.

57

4. Images

WITHIN WEEKS of Prince Albert's death, schemes to commemorate him were being considered by towns, cities and institutions throughout Great Britain. No previous individual had been so widely honoured. Although the death of Sir Robert Peel in 1850 and the heroic feats of Nelson and the Duke of Wellington had led to the erection of many local memorials (prompting one commentator to remark 'we are living in an age emphatically of statues and testimonials')[1] these were soon to be outnumbered by monuments to the Prince Consort.

Civic pride was a major factor in the proliferation of local memorials. The decision to erect these was taken in most instances at meetings called early in 1862 in response to circulars from the London committee requesting the town's financial assistance towards the National Memorial. It was suggested at these meetings that an individual municipal contribution would be lost in a national enterprise whereas a local memorial, as well as being an adornment to the town, would proclaim to future generations the esteem in which Prince Albert was held by its citizens. Objections were also raised to sending money to a memorial in the capital which the majority of the local inhabitants would never see. A competitive spirit between towns also made the movement to erect memorials to some extent self-generating, while many promotors felt obliged to put up a monument. The Master of Trinity implied, when he spoke of the enthusiasm to erect statues of Prince Albert even in places 'that were not connected with him at all', that it would be inexcusable for Cambridge University not to similarly honour its late Chancellor.[2]

Genuine feelings of sympathy and loyalty for the widowed Queen also promoted the movement for Albert memorials. One contemporary newspaper, surprised by the 'universality, spontaneity, and liberality' of the enthusiasm for statues, attributed 'the very general desire to perpetuate, in bronze and marble, the recollection of his great talents and virtues' to the 'inherent loyalty of the British people, and their affectionate admiration of the Queen, as well as to the sympathy awakened by the impressive suddenness of the Prince's death'.[3]

The schemes for local monuments seriously hampered efforts to raise money for the National Memorial. But, while The Times urged the provincial towns to sacrifice their individual projects, and merge their subscriptions with the languishing London fund,[4] journals like The Building News were of the opinion that the profusion of monuments would testify 'how universal was the affectionate respect for the Prince, and how widespread was his popularity'.[5]

Some of the provincial memorials to Prince Albert were gifts from private donors, and some were paid for directly out of institutional or municipal funds, but the majority were erected by public subscription. The task of collecting subscriptions, in the case of municipal memorials, and of determining the type of monument, was entrusted to a committee (or its sub-committees), usually under the chairmanship of the mayor, which was appointed at a public meeting. The precise form of monument selected was determined by a number of factors, of which cost was perhaps the most important, but about half the memorials erected to the Prince Consort comprised or incorporated an image of him.

The practice of commissioning a posthumous portrait, whether in the form of a painting, statue or bust, of an eminent person was encouraged from the 1830s by the cult of hero-worship, and the belief that art might fulfil an educational role. Thomas Carlyle, who had done so much to promote 'Hero Worship', was convinced of the power of 'Brazen and other Images' to influence the passer-by—for good or ill,[6] while Samuel Smiles, in *Self Help* (1859) related how Dr. Thomas Guthrie had been inspired in his own efforts for the Ragged School Movement by a picture of John Pounds, a humble cobbler, who had given shelter and instruction to orphans in Portsmouth.[7] This conviction that images of good men could inspire others, particularly of the working classes, undoubtedly lay behind endeavours to provide free admission to the monuments of national heroes in St. Paul's Cathedral and Westminster Abbey, the establishment in 1856 of the National Portrait Gallery (in which Carlyle played a prominent part), and the erection from about 1830 of increasing numbers of public statues of national and local worthies, past and present.

After his death the Prince Consort joined this pantheon of national heroes, and memorials incorporating an image of him were erected with this didactic function in mind. Statues were intended to remind people of 'his bright example and noble qualities', and to 'stimulate them and others in their own paths of duty'.[8] Queen Victoria herself expressed the hope that the figure of Prince Albert at Perth (Plate 72), for example, would encourage 'those of future generations to the practice of those virtues which have rendered the memory of her beloved and great husband so dear to the people of this country',[9] while a writer in *The British Workman* observed 'In by-gone times, it was not among the mighty and the noble that examples could be found to stimulate those whose inheritance was labour. No one would have thought of taking a working man by the hand, and leading him to the statue or picture of an illustrious Prince . . . and before that august representation to say, "Son of toil, behold this noble example", yet . . . this is what we say . . . of the late Prince Consort.'[10]

Accessibility was essential for a public monument to perform its didactic function, and it was perhaps partly for this reason that a greater number of Albert memorials took the form of a statue than of a picture. Painted portraits of the Prince tended to be commissioned as part of a larger memorial scheme (such as the one for Bridgwater Town Hall), or by companies and societies for the exclusive edification of their members. Thus, a posthumous portrait was subscribed for by members of the Honourable Artillery Company, of which Prince Albert had been Captain General and Colonel from 1843 until his death. Painted by J.G. Middleton, a member of the company, it was exhibited at the Royal Academy in 1862, and now hangs on the staircase in Armoury House.[11] In February 1862 the Cloth-workers' Company (whose new hall had been opened by Prince Albert in March 1860) voted to purchase full-length portraits of the Prince and the Queen. At Her Majesty's

Palace. The overall comp
Charlotte, which was re
theme of domestic educa
in the benefits to arts,
promotion of which thei

The paintings were ir
removed in 1922 and ar
Theed, is a version of the
the medallion portrait of
Wyon, includes an imag
Rowland Hill.[17]

Several other busts and
him, mainly by instituti
commissioned a marble
companion to the one of
placed in the Council Cl
World War.[18] The Dunc
Albert by John Steell for
placed a replica of Theed
Albert Room) in 1863;[20]
portrait medallion by Ti
a bust for the entrance ha
Albert's name. The mode
the wording of the inscri

suggestion, copies after Winterhalter's portraits of her and the Prince in their Garter robes were at first proposed, and W.'S. Herrick was commissioned in June to execute these for 250 guineas. The painter subsequently suggested that original pictures would be more suitable, and he offered to furnish these for 400 guineas. The offer was accepted, and the paintings were hung on the staircase in the Clothworkers' Hall until May 1941, when they were destroyed by fire following an air-raid.[12]

A more readily accessible portrait of the Prince Consort was that presented to the National Portrait Gallery by Queen Victoria (Plate 52). This was first offered in 1862, and again the Queen suggested a copy of a portrait by Winterhalter whose likenesses of Prince Albert she considered the best. The Trustees of the Gallery were anxious to receive a replica by the artist himself rather than a copy by another painter, but, because Winterhalter was known to be unwilling to undertake repetitions, they suggested that a bust might resolve the difficulty. The Queen, however, was keen to give a painting, and eventually a compromise was reached: Winterhalter would superintend an 'artist friend' making a replica of his 1859 portrait of Prince Albert in his uniform as Colonel of the Rifle Brigade 'so as to be able to call it a work of his own'. The painting was placed in the National Portrait Gallery in April 1867.[13]

A more elaborate commemorative scheme, of which a portrait of Prince Albert formed but one part, was adopted by the Royal Society of Arts. The Society's tribute to its late President at first consisted of a generous donation of £1,000 towards the National Monument. There was, however, a widespread feeling among members that the Society should have its own memorial also. Bowing to this pressure, the Council called a second General Meeting on 7 February 1863, at which it was resolved that a marble bust should be commissioned, and an Albert medal established to be awarded 'for distinguished merit in promoting Arts, Manufactures, and Commerce'. A subscription, limited to one guinea per member, was opened and by July 1863 nearly £700 had been collected. This was considerably more than was needed for the bust (estimated at £150) and it was decided to devote the surplus to the purchase of portraits for the Great Room of the Society's premises.

This room was decorated with six history paintings, executed by James Barry between 1777 and 1790, which were fitted between Gainsborough's *Lord Folkestone* on the west wall, and Reynolds's *Lord Romney* on the opposite wall. Barry had proposed that these two paintings should be replaced by a portrait of George III, and one of Queen Charlotte superintending the education of her children at Windsor Castle. There had been some opposition to this scheme, however, and the paintings had never been executed. The Society's Council now proposed to realise in some degree Barry's original intentions by substituting the portraits of Lords Romney and Folkestone by ones of Prince Albert and Queen Victoria, at an estimated cost of between 600 and 700 guineas.[14]

The portrait of Prince Albert by C.W. Cope (Plate 53) shows him in Garter robes, with the Charter of Incorporation of the 1851 Exhibition lying on the table by his side. The hourglass, and the weeping cherub with downturned torch, indicate the posthumous nature of the work. Cope recorded that Queen Victoria visited him in his studio to inspect the portrait, bringing with her 'a packet of photographs of the Prince', one of which she presented to the painter, and made 'some judicious criticisms'.[15] J.C. Horsley's companion picture of the Queen (Plate 54) depicts her with her children holding a plan of the Crystal

61

52. (*facing page*) F.X. Winterhalter: *Prince Albert*, National Portrait Gallery.

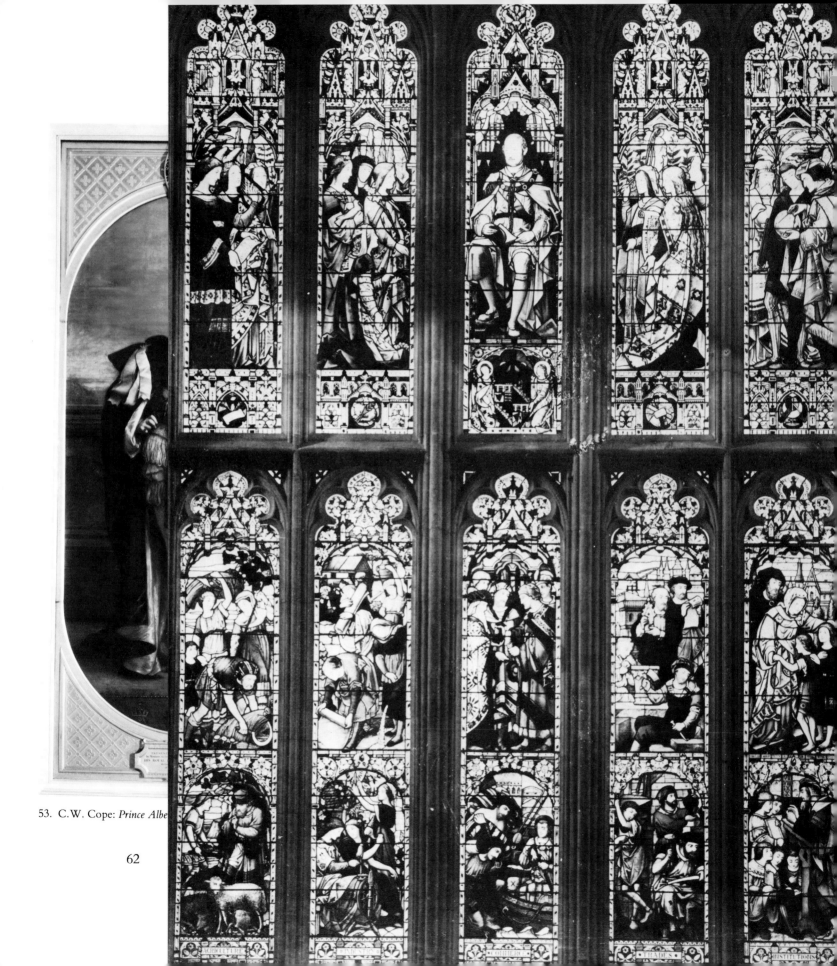

53. C.W. Cope: *Prince Albe...*

marble statue at Balmoral.[22] The Queen herself gave a replica of Theed's bust to Surrey County Hospital, Guildford, which was erected as a memorial to the late Prince.[23]

The Corporation of London's other memorial to the Prince Consort—a stained glass window in the west end of the Guildhall (Plate 57)—was also destroyed during the Second World War. This was intended to show 'the leading ideas and occupations of this country, on which the Prince brought to bear so much influence, and which derived such great advantages from his personal encouragement'.[24] The lower lights had figures symbolic of Agriculture, Industry, Trades, Institutions and Commerce; the upper ones, representations of Music, Poetry, History, Peace, Purity, Religion and Home Prosperity, Architecture, Painting, Sculpture, Science and Literature; and the two side wings had figures emblematic of Wisdom, Prudence, Justice and Fortitude. In the centre was a seated portrait of Prince Albert holding a book in one hand, while in the background two figures unveiled the 1851 Exhibition—his most conspicuous contribution to the encouragement of arts and sciences, trade and industry. The design, by Ward and Hughes, was selected by Queen Victoria from a short-list of six chosen from the seventy entries submitted in competition, but she declined an invitation from the Lord Mayor to unveil 'a mere memorial window', and the inauguration ceremony on 3 November 1870 was presided over by Prince Arthur instead.[25] Another window in memory of Prince Albert was presented to the Guildhall at York by George Leeman, a local Alderman, and unveiled by the Prince of Wales in 1866. It depicted the Prince Consort at a banquet given in his honour in the hall by the mayors of England and Wales in 1850, preliminary to the Great Exhibition. Executed by Hardman and Company to a design by J.E. Doyle, it too was destroyed during the Second World War.[26]

A considerable number of stained glass windows were also placed in churches as memorials to Prince Albert. This form of commemoration had become popular for public monuments because, in a devout age, they would be seen by large numbers of inhabitants. However, the placing of a work commemorating a secular hero within a church was open to 'objections and difficulties', particularly if the window were to be destined for the east end and a portrait of the deceased included.[27] For this reason, most of the Albert memorial windows took the form of biblical scenes which alluded to the Prince's charitable and Christian nature in some symbolic way. Thus, the east window of St. Mary's, Nottingham (Plate 56), by Hardman and Company, depicts incidents from the life of Christ which were also thought to be 'emblematical of the Reformatories, Schools, Hospitals, Asylums, and other similar institutions, which H.R.H. patronised; and of that general benevolence which he practised'. The only specific visual reference to Prince Albert in this, and in most of the other windows erected to him, is in the representation of his coat of arms.[28]

The memorial window executed by Clayton and Bell under Scott's supervision for the east end of St. George's Chapel, Windsor (Plate 58), overcame the problem of this form of monument by taking as its theme the Incarnation of Christ, and by connecting 'faithful service on earth *in* Christ, with reward in Heaven from Him'.[29] The window depicts passages from the life of Christ, with figures on either side representing faithful followers from the Old and New Testaments who were chosen because they furnished parallels with Prince Albert. More direct reference to the Prince Consort was made in the series of small medallions at the base of the window. These avoided 'objections and difficulties' by showing him as 'an ideal princely figure (not a portrait)'[30] engaged in various pursuits—

65

promoting agriculture, commerce, education, manufactures, and the arts, assisting the sick and poor, and with his family. These scenes demonstrated how 'the life and grace flowing from our blessed Lord Incarnate, bore such noble fruit' in Prince Albert, and the window as a whole was intended 'through the senses, to bring home to the heart one more true idea of the glory and tenderness of God, to stir up one deeper feeling of love, and thankfulness for an example so noble, to mould one life to more earnest walking after such a pattern of self-devotion . . . to cast one gleam of brightness and hope over sorrow, by its witness to a continuous life in Christ, in and beyond the grave'.[31] The window, which Queen Victoria described as 'really magnificent',[32] was installed in time for the Prince of Wales's wedding in March 1863.

Stained glass windows, like paintings and busts, were a comparatively inexpensive form of monument; that erected to Prince Albert at Christ Church, Banbury, for example, cost £50, while a more elaborate work at Trinity Church, Knaresborough, cost £270.[33] Where larger sums were collected, statues of the Prince were often preferred. Initial plans for the local memorial at Bristol, for example, had been for an elaborate monument incorporating a figure of the Prince, costing £3,000, but failure to raise this sum obliged the committee to lower its sights to a window in the cathedral for £1,000. Endeavours to raise sufficient subscriptions even for this proved unsuccessful, and the committee eventually abandoned all hopes for a local memorial, and sent 'between eighty and ninety pounds' to the national fund in December 1862.[34]

Although Bristol was disappointed in its scheme for a sculptural monument, over twenty-five statues of Prince Albert were erected in towns and cities throughout Britain and abroad, some of them in connection with buildings, but the majority as free-standing figures. Although public statues were a popular commemorative form by 1861, the number raised in memory of Prince Albert exceeded that to any previous individual. Indeed, the demand for statues of Prince Albert after his death prompted a resident of Warrington, concerned that his town was unable to afford its own figure, to suggest that one or two designs should be procured from leading sculptors such as J.H. Foley and W.C. Marshall, which could then be mass-produced in bronze and offered to the public for £250 each.[35] Cost was a primary consideration in determining what form of statue should be erected— a standing, seated or equestrian figure, either on its own or as the principal feature of a larger monument—but Queen Victoria's wishes occasionally influenced the decision. She also sometimes nominated the sculptor for the work, and advised and assisted artists in a number of ways. The Queen was most closely involved with the Scottish National Memorial to Prince Albert (Plate 59).

The scheme for this was officially launched at a public meeting held in Edinburgh on 19 March 1862, at which it was decided that the form and site of the monument should be determined by Queen Victoria.[36] The fund closed in January 1863 when it was estimated that about £12,000 would be available,[37] but, like that of the London memorial, the execution was protracted and fraught with difficulties.

Queen Victoria was at first enthusiastic about a design for a Gothic cross with statuary by the painter Joseph Noel Paton. The Committee, under the chairmanship of the Fifth Duke of Buccleuch, however, thought that it bore too close a resemblance to the memorial to the 1851 Exhibition, and also doubted whether it could be executed for the available

67

59. W. Simpson: *Unveiling of the Scottish National Memorial to Prince Albert, Edinburgh*, Royal Collection.

funds.[38] The Queen thereupon agreed to an open competition being held, and in March 1865 she selected a design for an equestrian monument by John Steell, the foremost Scottish sculptor of his day. This was to be erected on the Review Ground site in Queen's Park, Edinburgh.[39] The Committee later became concerned for its safety in this locality, 'in the vicinity of the lowest and worst of the population of the city' who might deface the memorial 'in drunken mischief or malevolence'.[40] They suggested that the monument should be erected instead on the site occupied by the fountain in front of Holyrood Palace where it could be protected by the guards.[41] Queen Victoria, however, rejected this location for one of the reasons why it had been considered appropriate: the fountain had been placed there by Prince Albert, and therefore could not be moved. She proposed that the memorial should be placed in Charlotte Square.[42] This was private property, but the residents who owned it were persuaded to give their consent by the Committee's promise to improve and embellish the square.[43]

The Committee was without the resources to pay for this remodelling, and was in financial difficulties anyway having decided to erect an elaborate and costly pedestal in red granite rather than the simple one in freestone originally proposed. Efforts both to raise further subscriptions and to secure a Government grant were unsuccessful, and it was not until the Duke of Buccleuch offered to guarantee the cost of the pedestal—a gesture which revived interest and prompted generous donations (including one of £300 from Princess

68

60. (*facing page*) D.W. Stevenson: *The Labouring Classes*, Scottish National Memorial to Prince Albert, Edinburgh.

Louise, who had married a Scot)—that the Committee was able to order the base, and that the work of remodelling the square could commence, in the summer of 1873.[44]

The problems of the Committee were not over. Steell estimated that the equestrian statue would be ready for the proposed inauguration by Queen Victoria in August 1874, but these hopes were dashed in March of that year when the head and forelegs of the horse were damaged during casting.[45] Though troubled by poor health, the sculptor succeeded in completing the work in time for the unveiling on 17 August 1876, but the exasperated Committee noted that he had caused unnecessary delay by insisting on completely remodelling the figure of the Prince.[46]

The memorial comprises an equestrian statue of the Prince in Field Marshal's uniform, executed under Queen Victoria's close supervision,[47] in which the horse and rider are in 'calm, quiescent repose'[48] as most befitting Prince Albert 'whose triumphs were sought in walks of peaceful industry and progress'.[49] The statue surmounts an elaborate pedestal (designed by the architect David Bryce) decorated with four bas-reliefs illustrating incidents in the life of the Prince—his marriage to Queen Victoria; with his family; distributing awards; and at the opening of the Great Exhibition. Beneath these reliefs are clusters of Prince Albert's heraldic and honorary emblems executed by William Brodie, and symbols of war and peace by Alexander Handyside Ritchie.[50] The most conspicuous features of the memorial are, however, the four groups executed by different sculptors on the angled projections of the base. These represent the upper classes, by Brodie, the labouring classes (Plate 60) and the arts and education (both by D.W. Stevenson),[51] and the services (Plate 61) by Clark Stanton. They were intended to 'express the admiration in which he [Prince Albert] was held by the whole people'. Some of the figures approach the statue of the Prince and, 'looking up to it with reverence and affection', leave at its base 'chaplets and wreaths, in token of their gratitude and love',[52] while others, such as the professor and the labourer's wife, are shown explaining the virtues and rewards of good men. The idea of figures paying homage to a departed worthy, or expounding his achievements to others, is not new in British monumental sculpture, but in earlier examples these tend to be allegorical representations. Steell rejected this convention because he considered it was unintelligible to the majority of people. Instead, he 'adopted the most direct and familiar mode of expression'—life-size figures in contemporary dress—'so that every grade may not only at once perceive, but *feel* the idea'.[53] This simple but compelling sentiment of homage, lucidly expressed in the realistic style of the figures, appealed to Queen Victoria who instructed General Grey to inform Steell how touched she had been by his design.[54] She no doubt hoped that the public would behave in the same way as the bronze figures.

National pride also prompted the people of Ireland to erect their own memorial to Prince Albert (Plate 62), but nationalistic feeling put the scheme at risk. The project was launched at a meeting held in the Mansion House, Dublin, on 15 March 1862, and by October of that year about £6,000 had been promised.[55] The proceedings were impeded, as at Edinburgh, by the difficulty of finding a suitable site. It was hoped initially that the monument would be erected on St. Stephen's Green in Dublin, then private property, which would be opened to the public as the Albert Park, but a Bill to transfer the administration of the site to the Commissioner of Woods and Forests was defeated in 1863.[56] The committee then secured a site on College Green[57] but when, in November 1865,

70

62. (*left*) J.H. Foley: *Irish National Memorial to Prince Albert*, Dublin.

63. J.E. Thomas: *Welsh National Memorial to Prince Albert*, Tenby.

it came to their notice that the Government were proposing to convert Leinster Lawn behind the Royal Dublin Society House into a public garden, they lost no time in seeking Queen Victoria's approval for the memorial to be erected there instead. This site, between the National Gallery and Museum, was felt to be the most appropriate, and had been considered earlier but abandoned because the Committee feared that the Royal Dublin Society, who owned the land, would restrict public access, 'allowing only (unless upon stated occasions, and by grace especial) a peep through a gaunt, tasteless railing into the *sanctum sanctorum*'.[58] The committee was supported in its application to the Queen by Henry Cole, who pointed out that on Leinster Lawn the memorial would be under the control of the Government rather than the Dublin municipal authorities, and would thereby be protected from any 'odd turn' of 'Irish humour' such as that which had caused the statue of William III to be reversed on its pedestal.[59] Queen Victoria agreed to this change of site, but Cole was proved to be sadly over-confident about the memorial's safety from Fenian outrage.

The Queen, who declined an invitation to attend the unveiling despite suggestions that her visit would have 'a very material effect in checking Fenianism & disloyalty',[60] sent Prince Alfred, Duke of Edinburgh, in her place. The ceremony was scheduled for 6 June 1872, but on 20 April the sculptor of the memorial, J.H. Foley, informed the committee that owing to the wetness of the season, it had proved impossible to excavate the stone for the pedestal. The committee promptly arranged for a temporary base to be erected, but a further communication from Foley on 23 May brought the news that as a result of an explosion in the foundry of Messrs. Prince and Co., in which the principal workman had been severely injured, the statue of Prince Albert would not be completed in time. Undaunted, the resourceful committee thereupon secured the full-size plaster model of the statue from the sculptor. This was placed on the temporary pedestal, together with the completed bronze figures representing Art, Science, Agriculture and Industry around the base, in time for the Duke of Edinburgh to inspect, but not unveil, the work on 6 June.[61] Three days later, Fenians attempted to blow it up. Fortunately the powder was badly placed, and only slight damage was caused to the cloak and to the feet, with one of the rosettes being lost from the slipper.[62] It was perhaps to forestall another act of vandalism that the completed monument was never ceremonially unveiled.

Nationalistic sentiments were expressed more subtly in the Welsh memorial to Prince Albert (Plate 63). The Mayor of Tenby decided early in 1864 that Wales should follow the lead of England, Scotland and Ireland and erect its own national memorial.[63] (The committee later increased the size of the statue from seven to eight feet so that it would be 'equal to those about to be erected at Dublin and Edinburgh'.)[64] The commission for the marble statue of Prince Albert in Field Marshal's uniform beneath the Garter cloak, was entrusted to the Welsh sculptor, John Evan Thomas. It was erected on a pedestal of native limestone designed by a local architect, H. Maule Ffinch, which is decorated with national emblems and inscriptions partly in Welsh. The back panel, for example, shows the royal monogram within an escutcheon supported by a 'semi-recumbent but still resilient leek'[65] and a rampant red dragon of Cadwaladr with the motto 'Anordifygol Ddraig Cymru' ('The Dragon of Wales is invincible'). The memorial was erected on Castle Hill, Tenby, and was unveiled by Prince Arthur, then only fifteen years old, on 2 August 1865.

The Tenby monument, which cost £2,250, is not so ambitious or elaborate as the other national memorials, nor indeed as some of the statues erected in provincial towns. Of these, five were equestrian portraits—a surprisingly large number considering that original works of this type were expensive, costing between £5,000 and £6,000. An equestrian statue was a well-established form for the representation of monarchs and princes, since it emphasised their superior status, but it was also thought to embody military overtones which were considered by some to be inappropriate for monuments to the Prince Consort. Although a Field Marshal, and connected with several regiments, Prince Albert's most conspicuous achievements had been in the arts of peace, not war. Accordingly, 'as illustrating his character and life', a writer in *The Glasgow Citizen* concluded, an equestrian statue 'must be altogether a failure'.[66] Queen Victoria, however, showed some predilection for this form, selecting Steell's design for the Scottish National Memorial, and proposing an equestrian figure by Marochetti for the monument in Glasgow (Plate 66)[67]—a decision prompted in part, no doubt, by the fact that the sculptor had already executed a similar statue of herself there. Nonetheless, a local newspaper regretted that 'the gentle, science-loving, and unwarlike husband of our Gracious Queen' was to be represented on horse-back.[68] Similarly, Thomas Thornycroft secured the commission for the Wolverhampton memorial (Plate 65) by assuring the committee of the Queen's preference for equestrian statues of the Prince Consort.[69]

The provincial equestrian statues of Albert do not depict a warlike Prince but, like Steell's figure crowning the Scottish National Memorial, they avoid military overtones by adopting a reposeful image appropriate to the Prince Consort's character and pursuits.

64. Thomas Thornycroft: *Prince Albert*, Liverpool.

65. Thomas Thornycroft: *Prince Albert*, Wolverhampton.

66. Carlo Marochetti: *Prince Albert*, Glasgow.

67. Charles Bacon: *Prince Albert*, Holborn Circus.

Thomas Thornycroft, in his equestrian statue commissioned by Liverpool Corporation for £5,000, sought to overcome the objections to this type by depicting 'a philosophical prince rather than an honorary soldier' (Plate 64).[70] Prince Albert is shown as he most frequently appeared in public, wearing frock coat and trousers rather than military dress, and holding a hat by his side as though in the act of saluting the people during an official visit. The statue was unveiled outside St. George's Hall on 10 October 1866. It was regarded as 'one of the most faithful and characteristic likenesses yet produced' because Thornycroft had been personally acquainted with the Prince Consort and professionally employed by him for many years.[71] It was for this reason that versions of the statue were commissioned as memorials at Halifax and Wolverhampton,[72] and also because repetitions were comparatively cheap: the Halifax statue cost 1,300 guineas, and the Wolverhampton figure £1,200. The former was erected at Ward's End in Halifax on 17 September 1864 and, except for the scroll which replaces the hat held in the right hand, is a replica of the Liverpool work.[73] In the version for Wolverhampton (Plate 65), however, Queen Victoria instructed Thornycroft to depict her husband in military dress, and lent him Prince Albert's Field Marshal's uniform for the purpose. She also lent him the Prince's saddle cloth, granted him access to the royal stables, and visited him in his studio on several occasions.[74] Despite Thornycroft's generalisation of the uniform compared with Steell's more detailed treatment, a writer in *The Building News* pronounced it to be totally inappropriate because 'it was as a civilian that he [Prince Albert] was familiar to the view, as he was endeared to the hearts of the people'.[75] The statue was unveiled by Queen Victoria on 30 November 1866.

Marochetti's statue in George Square, Glasgow (Plate 66) also shows the Prince in Field Marshal's uniform, seated on a horse which steps forward. The figure is rather stiff and formal, but the likeness was commended, and the group as a whole praised for embodying

75

68. G.H. Thomas: *Unveiling of the statue of Prince Albert at Coburg*, Royal Collection.

'the calm, simple, and at the same time dignified nature of the subject'.[76] The pursuits of the Prince are recorded in the bas-reliefs on two sides of the pedestal illustrative of Industrial Arts and Fine Arts. A similar arrangement was adopted by Charles Bacon in his more spirited equestrian monument at Holborn Circus, London (Plate 67), unveiled by the Prince of Wales on 9 January 1874. This shows the Prince Consort in Field Marshal's uniform seated on a prancing charger, raising his hat in salutation. The base is decorated with bas-reliefs depicting the Prince laying the foundation stone of the Royal Exchange, and Britannia distributing awards at the Great Exhibition. At either end is placed a partially-draped female figure, one representing History, and the other, Peace. These are examples of the attenuated allegorical figures which adorn many mid-nineteenth-century monuments, but which both Steell and Foley had rejected in favour of contemporary figures realistically treated, in the Scottish and Irish National Memorials.

The most popular form of Albert memorial statue was the single standing figure. This was also the cheapest and, unlike equestrian figures, could be supplied to suit the financial constraints of any fund simply by varying the material employed. Thus, Woolner's Caen-stone figure in Oxford University Museum cost £300 (Plate 78), and William Brodie's freestone statue at Perth cost £280 (Plate 72), while Matthew Noble charged £1,100 for his marble figure at Salford (Plate 75), and J.H. Foley received £1,620 for his more elaborate statue on a base enriched with bas-reliefs for Cambridge University (Plate 74). Marble and stone were preferred for standing figures (even those placed outdoors) not only because they were cheaper, but also because of a prevailing prejudice against bronze. It was felt by some that this material was only suited to colossal works because it did not permit the reproduction of details, and that it tended to render the statue a black silhouette against the sky. J.E. Thomas, for example, advised the Mayor of Tenby to avoid bronze because it looked heavy, and dwarfed everything around it. He suggested that a figure of Prince Albert in Sicilian marble, which was 'light, and as hard as metal', would look 'much less common' than one in bronze.[77]

Bronze was more expensive than marble if a new work was commissioned but, as

76

Thornycroft's statues have demonstrated, once a model existed, replicas could be executed comparatively cheaply. In fact, all the metal standing figures of Prince Albert were casts after two models: William Theed's bronze statue at Coburg (Plate 68), and Joseph Durham's electrotype figure surmounting the memorial to the Great Exhibition of 1851 (Plate 1). The firm of Elkington's offered replicas of both of these works to the Tenby Committee for between £500 for an electrotype, and £1,000 for a bronze.[78]

The models of Theed and Durham were popular for other reasons too. Both sculptors had been closely associated with Prince Albert during his lifetime, and were thus considered eminently qualified to produce a good likeness of him after his death. The particular advantages enjoyed by Theed, in having been the sculptor to take the Prince's deathmask and in having been selected by Queen Victoria to execute so many of her memorials to Prince Albert, were generally recognised. *The Times*, for example, describing the inauguration of Theed's statue of the Prince at Coburg, observed that these advantages had allowed the sculptor 'again and again to reproduce the most perfect likeness of a countenance so familiar to all of us'.[79] This statue shows the Prince in Garter robes holding a Field Marshal's

69. Inauguration of the Royal Albert Infirmary, Bishop's Waltham, from *The Illustrated London News*, 18 November 1865.

baton and a plan of the Great Exhibition. It was presented to Coburg by Queen Victoria—a fact which is recorded by the medallion portrait of her on the half-column by his right side. The Queen described the statue as 'beautiful & so like'[80] when she unveiled it in 1865, and suggested a replica for the memorial at Sydney, Australia, because she felt that 'the very best likeness of the beloved & great Prince should be sent to so distant part of the world'.[81] This bronze repetition was unveiled at the entrance of Hyde Park, Sydney, on 23 April 1866.[82] The Queen's warm approbation of the likeness, and her supervision of the execution of the Coburg figure, no doubt encouraged Sir E.W. Watkin to order another bronze replica for presentation to Grimsby in 1879,[83] and Frederick Perkins to commission a reduced terracotta version as a gift for the Royal Albert Infirmary at Bishop's Waltham in 1865 (Plate 69).[84]

Similar advantages surrounded Joseph Durham's statue of Prince Albert in the robes of the Order of the Bath, which surmounts the memorial of the 1851 Exhibition (Plate 1). This was the first posthumous figure of the Prince to be completed, and was executed under the close scrutiny of the Queen. The position of the right arm, habitual to the Prince, was determined by her,[85] for example, and she pronounced the completed statue 'a fine successful one'[86] when she inspected it privately on 9 June 1863, the day before the official unveiling. Royal approval of the work prompted the mayor of Birmingham to suggest that a replica should be secured for the town's memorial to the Prince Consort. It would be a great honour to Birmingham, he stated, to erect a copy of a statue which the Queen had approved for a national memorial—and it would cost £500 less than any comparable figure because the model existed.[87] Replicas of Durham's work were considered by other towns,[88] but in the event only one was erected—at St. Peter Port, Guernsey, which was unveiled on 8 October 1863. Another version, in which court shoes were substituted for the 'Robin Hood style' boots which one commentator thought 'the only objectionable part' of the original figure,[89] was presented to the Albert Middle Class College, Framlingham, Suffolk, by one of its founders, Sir Thomas Lucas, in 1865 (Plate 70).

Several of the other standing statues of Prince Albert depict him in state robes, and some of these seem to have been influenced by the 'approved' designs of Theed and Durham. Certainly R.L. Boulton's figure, commissioned in August 1864[90] for the memorial column designed by John Gibbs at Abingdon, bears a close resemblance to Durham's statue. Indeed, the whole monument, which was unveiled on 22 June 1865 (Plate 71), appears an attenuated, Gothic version of the memorial to the 1851 Exhibition. William Brodie's statue of Prince Albert in his robes of the Order of the Thistle, erected at Perth in 1864 (Plate 72), was also commissioned after the unveiling of the 1851 memorial.[91] The Prince is shown in a similar pose to that in Durham's figure, and holds a plan of the Exhibition building against a column in a manner reminiscent of Theed's work. The sculptor received assistance from Prince Alfred who twice visited Brodie's studio in Edinburgh and suggested improvements to the likeness and the costume.[92] Analogous poses occur in Matthew Noble's figure for the Manchester monument, and in J.E. Thomas's statue for the Welsh National Memorial (Plate 63), executed 'according to the Queen's express commands, and afterwards personally revised by Her Majesty'.[93] J.H. Foley's statue of the Prince in Garter robes in the Council House, Birmingham, unveiled in 1868, is a more reposeful version of this type (Plate 73).

70. Joseph Durham: *Prince Albert*, Framlingham College.

71. Inauguration of the Albert Memorial, Abingdon, from *The Illustrated London News*, 1 July 1865.

72. William Brodie: *Prince Albert*, Perth.

73. J.H. Foley: *Prince Albert*, Birmingham, Council House.

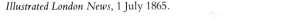

74. J.H. Foley: *Prince Albert*, Madingley, Cambridge.

75. Matthew Noble: *Prince Albert*, Salford.

Foley's statue for Cambridge University (Plate 74) shows Prince Albert in his robes as Chancellor of that institution. The drapery swathes around the figure in the manner of a classical toga.[94] The statue surmounts a pedestal decorated with bas-reliefs illustrative of those subjects which he strove to encourage—Art, Literature and Science. It was unveiled in the Fitzwilliam Museum in 1878, but is now at Madingley, just outside Cambridge. Although he had not executed a likeness of him during his lifetime, Foley had been held in high regard by Prince Albert, and Queen Victoria commended the Cambridge figure as 'simple and dignified'.[95]

The Prince Consort is represented in his robes as Chancellor of Cambridge University in other statues which were erected in connection with buildings devoted to educational purposes. Thus E.B. Stephens employed them in the Caen-stone figure he donated in 1870 to the Royal Albert Memorial Museum in his native Exeter (Plate 82), and so did Matthew Noble in his statue of the Prince unveiled in the forecourt of the Peel Park Museum and Library, Salford, on 7 November 1864 (Plate 75).[96] Prince Albert is shown holding a scroll in allusion to his abilities as an orator, while a long passage from one of his speeches is inscribed on the pedestal. The pile of books and the globe on the base indicate his scientific and scholarly interests, and are examples of the devices widely used in mid-nineteenth-century public sculpture to denote the office or pursuits of the person commemorated.

Noble was a popular sculptor, and he executed statues of the Prince Consort not only for Salford and Manchester, but also for Leeds Town Hall (1865), where Prince Albert is similarly represented as an orator, and for the Victoria and Albert Museum, Bombay, unveiled in 1872 (Plate 76)[97]. Here, he is appropriately dressed in the robes of the Order of the Star of India, while the base is enriched with two female seated figures symbolising Art and Science, subjects in which Prince Albert showed particular interest, emphasised by the inscription, taken from Tennyson's dedication to the *Idylls of the King*, 'dear to Science, dear to Art'. It was stated that Queen Victoria had 'anxiously watched' the progress of the figure, 'courteously offering suggestions to Mr. Noble in order that it might be an exact a resemblance as possible of her lamented husband',[98] but the Queen, on the whole, did not consider the sculptor's busts and statues of Prince Albert 'very like—certainly not characteristic likenesses'.[99]

The robes of the different orders of chivalry to which Prince Albert belonged, and of his office as Chancellor of Cambridge University, circumvented many of the renowned problems of dress in nineteenth-century portrait sculpture. Although contemporary costume had largely superseded classical dress for public statues of great men by this date, the frock coat and trousers were considered by many to be inelegant and unsculpturesque. Moreover, figures in which modern clothes were adopted were thought to perpetuate 'the whimsical and the ephemeral fashion of the day',[100] rather than the more enduring intellectual attainments of the person commemorated. Official dress was one solution to this problem, and no doubt explains why most sculptors opted for state or Chancellor's

76. Matthew Noble: *Prince Albert*, Victoria and Albert Museum, Bombay.

robes, or Field Marshal's uniform, in their statues of Prince Albert. Chancellor's robes effectively disguised the irregular outline of the civilian dress habitually worn underneath, and created an impressive and unified silhouette. Similarly, the mantle of the various orders insured 'more graceful folds'[101] than modern frock coat and trousers. Moreover, state robes were thought to display admirably 'the full, manly, and well-proportioned figure of the Prince'.[102] However, some objections were voiced. Noble, for example, was criticised for depicting the Prince in Chancellor's robes in the Salford statue because it was a dress 'in which he was seldom seen'.[103] Another writer, while recognising that Foley had probably adopted Garter robes in his Birmingham statue because of the 'angularity' of modern dress, stated that as Prince Albert had so emphatically embraced the 'spirit and tendencies' of the nineteenth century, he should have been represented in clothes typical of his age, and habitual to him. The writer also regretted the laborious reproduction of the tassels and ribbons ('unsightly excrescences') of the chosen robes.[104] F.T. Palgrave criticised Durham's figure crowning the 1851 memorial for incongruously showing the Prince, whose life and manners had been characterised by simplicity and earnestness, under masses of heavy robes and court decorations, which distracted attention from the portrait.[105] The writer likewise ridiculed Durham's 'robed and tasselled effigy' for Framlingham.[106] Only a few sculptors attempted to represent Prince Albert in ordinary attire, one of whom was Thomas Thornycroft in his Liverpool and Halifax statues (Plate 64).

The committee of the Licensed Victuallers' Association, when commissioning a statue in memory of its former patron, instructed the sculptor Thomas Earle to represent the Prince Consort in the civilian clothes which he had worn when he had laid the foundation stone of the new Albert wing of their Asylum in Kennington in 1858.[107] The statue (Plate 77), which was unveiled by the Prince of Wales on 9 August 1864, shows Prince Albert in frock coat and trousers, holding a scroll in his right hand, and resting his left on his cloak draped over a half-column, another common device in mid-nineteenth-century public monuments. A repetition of the figure, inaugurated in Pearson Park, Hull, on 14 October 1868, was commended for avoiding 'Royal robes' and 'the costume of a past antiquity', and for giving instead 'a true and faithful likeness of the Prince as he lived amongst us'. Earle's device of draping the cloak over the column, thereby disguising the angularity of the frock coat, was particularly applauded.[108] Nonetheless, the image is a fairly conventional example of mid-nineteenth-century treatment of a figure in contemporary dress.

A more original interpretation is evident in Thomas Woolner's statue, unveiled in Oxford University Museum in April 1864 (Plate 78). This figure also illustrates a typical incident in the Prince's public career, and shows him, dressed in frock coat and trousers beneath the short riding cloak he frequently wore, departing from a town he has just visited. 'There has been no attempt, on the part of the sculptor', *The Morning Post* commented, 'to shed around his work any elaborate appearance of princely grandeur, which the high rank of the original might, probably, have suggested to an artist of less legitimate pretensions, but his prevailing object has been to present a natural, life-like portraiture, unaided by any meretricious ornamentation.'[109] The unaffected and original pose of the figure, the use of modern dress and absence of any conventional devices is in marked contrast to the rather more stereo-typed images of Prince Albert in state or official robes.

82

77. Thomas Earle: *Prince Albert*, Licensed Victuallers' Garden Village, Denham, Buckinghamshire.

78. Thomas Woolner: *Prince Albert*, Oxford University Museum.

79. Carlo Marochetti: Model for the statue of Prince Albert at Aberdeen.

The type of dress employed was just one of several criticisms of Marochetti's statue of Prince Albert at Aberdeen. *The Aberdeen Herald*, for example, objected to the inconsistency of showing him holding a scroll in allusion to the speech he delivered to the British Association for the Advancement of Science at Aberdeen in 1859, while at the same time dressed in Field Marshal's uniform which he had not worn on that occasion. This was probably, however, an attempt to play down the military overtones apparent in the model where he is shown with a sword (Plate 79). Moreover, 'the military trappings and ribbands and bell-pull tassels and ornamental frippery', and the 'spread-eagle attitude' of the figure were regarded as alien to 'the quiet though earnest thoughtfulness and chastened unobtrusive dignity of the Prince'.[110] Other reviewers also thought that the figure, sunk in the chair, and dwarfed by boots and the mantle of the Order of the Thistle ('oppressed by wardrobe and upholstery' was one contemporary description)[111] failed to recall his 'full princely form',[112] and detracted from the portrait. This was considered a poor likeness, and the feeling prevailed that Marochetti should have designed a standing, rather than a seated, figure. Indeed, local dissatisfaction with the work was so intense that a movement to commission a marble standing figure of the Prince from William Brodie was started, although nothing came of this.[113]

Marochetti's monument is unimpressive, and the difficulties of rendering the seated pose in a dignified manner, together with the higher cost of a statue of this type compared with a standing figure, may partly explain why only three memorials to Prince Albert took this form.[114] However, Queen Victoria, who unveiled the statue on 13 October 1863, considered it 'a vy fine one',[115] and that Marochetti had been 'most successful with the likeness.'[116] Nonetheless, she was clearly aware of local criticism (the only occasion on which it was so forcibly expressed in relation to a statue of Prince Albert), and sought the Crown Princess's views. The latter reassured her mother that she could not 'see anything about it to find fault with' except, perhaps, the footstool, which she thought should have had a rim or feet to make it a 'better-looking object'. But this was merely 'a trifling detail', and her overall opinion was that Marochetti's figure was 'very fine, very dignified and noble'.[117]

84

5. Worldly Goods

ALTHOUGH it was hoped that statues of the Prince Consort would prove an inspiration to passers-by, such monuments served no purpose in the strictly utilitarian sense, any more than did the National Albert Memorial despite its meticulous didactic sculptural programme. It was left to private enterprise to realise the 'work of utility' initially proposed as part of the National Memorial—the Royal Albert Hall (Plate 80). The inscription records that this building, opened in 1871, 'was erected for the advancement of the arts and sciences and works of industry of all nations in fulfillment of the intention of Albert Prince Consort'. The idea originated as part of Prince Albert's grand plan for an educational complex on the South Kensington estate bought for the purpose by the 1851 Commissioners with the profits from the Great Exhibition. After the Prince Consort's death the scheme was nurtured by Henry Cole, and was finally made possible by the sale of debenture seats for life admissions to the Hall.

Both Cole's aim and his method of accomplishing it were regarded with suspicion and ran into fierce criticism. *The Saturday Review* complained that 'Of South Kensingtonism quintessential, void of science and of art, and rank with job, the type and climax is the Albert Hall, that monstrous cross between the Colosseum and a Yorkshire pie, warranted to do honour to the Prince Consort's memory by the variety of the entertainments provided and by the abundant dividend promised to its shareholders.'[1] Similarly, the towns which chose to commemorate the Prince Consort in a way which would be of practical use to their inhabitants, laid themselves open to the charge of self-interest, but this did little to check the spate of 'institutes, hospitals, almshouses, clock turrets, church spires, and an endless multiplicity of useful objects and purposes, all excellent and desirable in their way ... and most of them urged as precisely what Prince Albert himself would have wished, could he have been consulted'.[2]

A number of these memorial schemes were consciously in the 'South Kensington' tradition, and took the form of museums, schools and colleges. At the South Kensington (now the Victoria and Albert) Museum itself a Prince Consort Gallery (Plate 81) was set up where a ceramic mosaic portrait of Prince Albert (designed by Godfrey Sykes and executed by Cole's daughter Letitia) surveyed 'many of the most interesting and costly possessions of the Museum'.[3] The Devon Albert Memorial in Exeter was intended to house a school of art and science, a library and reading room as well as displays of natural history and antiquities—an ambitious (and expensive) undertaking which took several years to complete. Designed by John Hayward in the Gothic style, the building was begun in 1865 but was still incomplete three years later when the museum was opened (Plate 82). The statue

80. Francis Fowke and Henry Scott: The Royal Albert Hall, South Kensington.

81. (*right*) John Watkins: *The Prince Consort Gallery*, Victoria and Albert Museum.

of Prince Albert by E. B. Stephens was placed in a niche above the grand staircase.[4] Albert Institutes were put up at Dundee and Windsor,[5] and in Weston-super-Mare an Albert Memorial Hall and Museum was erected at a cost of £550. This building also housed an Albert Memorial School which opened in July 1863.[6]

In Suffolk it was felt that 'a School or College for the Scientific and Practical Instruction of the Middle Classes at a moderate cost would well accord with the views of the illustrious Prince and would be of permanent benefit to the County', and on 27 May 1863 the foundation-stone was laid of 'The Albert Middle Class College in Suffolk', now known as Framlingham College. The building was designed by Frederick Peck and the school opened on 10 April 1865. To mark the occasion, Sir Thomas Lucas, one of the founders, presented the statue of the Prince Consort by Joseph Durham which stands on an Aberdeen granite pedestal in front of the main entrance (Plate 70).[7] Albert Memorial Schools were put up in Collyhurst, Manchester, the gift of Sir Oswald Mosley; and in Birkenhead, the Albert Memorial Industrial Schools, designed by David Walker, were paid for by Sir William Jackson (Plate 83). The foundation-stone of the latter was laid in 1864, and on 24 October 1866 the school was opened 'for the education, industrial training, and maintenance, in whole or in part, of children who, through poverty, parental neglect, or any other cause, are left without instruction, or are in danger of contamination from vicious or criminal associates'. Despite the bust of Prince Albert over the entrance, within ten years the man in whose honour the school had been founded was all but forgotten, and it was commented that 'For many years to come ... the Birkenhead Industrial Schools will remain a monument of the benevolence and large-heartedness of the worthy founder, and the name of Sir William Jackson will be ever cherished in grateful remembrance by all these outcast children who may have the good fortune to be brought within the walls of the institution.'[8]

This was not the only example of an enterprise whose association with the Prince Consort quickly faded from memory. Few people today are aware that Bridgwater Town Hall was built in memory of Prince Albert,[9] but 'the idea of erecting it first occured at the death of the late Prince Consort ... and it was determined to build a Memorial Hall in commemoration of the man who has been so justly styled "Albert the Good". Bridgwater

82. John Hayward: Royal Albert Memorial Museum, Exeter.

83..David Walker: The Albert Memorial Industrial Schools, Birkenhead, from *The Illustrated London News*, 29 April 1865.

84. Paley and Austin: Royal Albert Hospital, Lancaster, from *The Illustrated London News*, 20 May 1876.

being at that time sadly deficient in having a place sufficiently commodious to hold public meetings in, it was thought that, whilst subserving to the public good, it would be a graceful act to associate Prince Albert's name with the building.'[10] Small wonder that *The Builder* remarked that 'A set of people *want* this or that; and forthwith they tack on to their real requirement a *false pretence* of erecting it *to the memory* of a popular Prince'.[11]

Four new hospitals were erected in memory of the Prince Consort, at Bishop's Waltham (Plate 69),[12] Guildford,[13] Lancaster (Plate 84)[14]—and at Wollongong, Australia[15]. Other existing hospitals were enlarged in his memory—Clayton Hospital at Wakefield, for example, in 1863,[16] and the Bath Royal United Hospital in 1864-8.[17] In Chesterfield it was suggested that a row of model cottages should be erected, and that the income from rent should be given to the local hospital, but support for the scheme withered under a barrage of criticism in the national press to the effect that 'if the Chesterfield people wish to aid the Chesterfield hospital' they should 'do it in a straightforward way, and not under the false pretence of erecting a memorial in honour of the dead'.[18] This plan did not materialise, but similar projects were carried out elsewhere. The Butchers' Charitable Institution (of which Prince Albert had been a patron) erected almshouses at Welham Green, Hertfordshire, which were opened in September 1863[19]. In Gravesend the Albert Memorial Endowment Fund was set up in February 1862. The townspeople hoped to raise £500 which would then be invested, and the interest distributed annually among the inhabitants of St. Thomas's Almshouses. In fact only £355 was raised, but the endowment was made and recorded by the trustees on a marble tablet on the building.[20] Larger towns, such as Cambridge, could afford to put up new almshouses in memory of the Prince Consort, and at Bagshot, an Albert Orphan Asylum was established, the foundation stone of which was laid by Queen Victoria.

Practical Christianity was represented by almshouses, but some monuments to Prince Albert took the form of pious gestures within the church itself. In addition to stained glass windows, Albert bells were installed at Clyst St. George, Devon, and Adelaide, Australia (a form of commemoration which *The Builder* thought should be imitated in every parish);[21] a screen was put up in Wellington College Chapel; and memorial tablets were also erected. One, with a medallion by Marochetti, was placed in St. Thomas's, Newport, Isle of Wight (Plate 85)—a tribute similar to Queen Victoria's at nearby Whippingham (Plate 19). The Queen presented figures of herself and Prince Albert, executed by Theodore

88

Phyffers, which were erected on the west front of Canterbury Cathedral in 1868 (Plate 86).[22] Sir Oswald Mosley paid for a church at Collyhurst, originally to be dedicated to St. Ann, but which became the Albert Memorial Church.[23]

Attaching Prince Albert's name to works which would in any case have been carried out, was the cheapest possible way of commemorating him. Like the church at Collyhurst, several Albert bridges (including that spanning the Thames) come into this category, as, of course, do innumerable Albert Roads, Streets and Terraces. There are several dozen of these in London alone, and no provincial town can be without at least one. Some of these were existing streets which simply underwent a change of name. At Stamford, for example, Terra Cotta Lane leading to a new footbridge over the River Welland (which had been opened in 1863 and soon after had come to be called the Albert Bridge) was re-named Albert Road.[24] Existing buildings also assumed a connection with the Prince Consort. The Smiths' Arms in Barnstaple, for example, lost its link with craft tradition and became 'The Albert' after the Prince's death.

Streets and public houses incorporating 'Albert' in their title pose two problems for the historian. Firstly, the date at which some works of this nature were called 'Albert' is difficult to document precisely, and it is clear that some were named after him during his lifetime. Secondly, it is not always possible to be certain that the 'Albert' referred to is the Prince Consort, for his eldest son, although he later became Edward VII, was also a Prince Albert, and was known as Albert Edward when Prince of Wales. Thus, some 'Albert' roads and public houses may have been called after the Prince of Wales (just as 'Prince Albert' tobacco was named after the future Edward VII, not the Prince Consort).[25]

Few purely architectural public monuments were erected, and these were often the result of expediency. In 1863 the portico of Barnard Castle railway station was moved, at the expense of the Saltburn Improvement Company, to the Valley Gardens in Saltburn, North Yorkshire, where it was termed the 'Albert Temple'.[26] It had long been customary to put up temporary triumphal arches for a royal visit to a town, and in Fettercairn, Grampian, it was decided to commemorate one such visit of Victoria and Albert in September 1861, by erecting a permanent arch. When the Prince died at the end of the year, it was decided to continue the scheme as an Albert memorial. The arch, designed by John Milne in the Gothic style, was completed in 1865 (Plate 87).[27]

Two obelisks were erected in honour of the Prince Consort—one at Balmoral, presented

85. (*far left*) Carlo Marochetti: Monument to Prince Albert, St. Thomas's Church, Newport, Isle of Wight.

86. Theodore Phyffers: *Prince Albert* and *Queen Victoria*, Canterbury Cathedral.

87. John Milne: Albert Memorial Arch, Fettercairn, Grampian.   88. The Albert Memorial, Mold, from a lithograph published in 1874

to the Queen by her tenantry on the estate there (perhaps in recognition of her first expressed wish for the form the National Memorial should take), and the other at Swanage, Dorset, in 1862. This scheme was proposed by George Burt, a Westminster builder, and the design has been identified as a copy of the obelisks in memory of two Lord Mayors, Robert Waithman and John Wilkes, which then stood on the site of the future Ludgate Circus in London, near where Burt had recently been repaving Fleet Street.[28]

The two obelisks in memory of London Lord Mayors did service as lamp standards in the new Ludgate Circus. In some cases, promoters of Albert memorial schemes sought a happier compromise between the interests of those who were in favour of practical, and those who preferred purely ornamental, monuments. Several Albert Memorials were intended to combine beauty and utility in the form of structures which performed some useful function, such as clock-towers, gas-lamps, and drinking fountains. At Mold, Clwyd, all three were combined in a monument, in bronzed cast-iron, which paid more attention to utility than to beauty despite being described, at its inauguration in September 1865, as 'a very conspicuous and attractive ornament' and 'a beautiful work of art' (Plate 88).[29] On two sides of the fountain at the base were circular panels containing profile heads of the Prince Consort, whilst the other two carried the taps. Between four cast-iron angels on top of this rose a pillar supporting the clock, which was illuminated by the gas-lamps. It was not long before this extraordinary monument 'was deemed an obstruction to the thorough-fare, and a resort of idlers', and it was taken down in 1884.[30]

A more imposing Albert Memorial, serving the same functions as that in Mold, was erected in Hastings in 1862-3. The design, by Edward A. Heffer of Liverpool 'in the Perpendicular style', was chosen as a result of a competition held in 1862. It took the form of a clock-tower with a drinking fountain at its base and four ornamental lamps at the corners. A Portland stone statue of the Prince, by Edwin Stirling, was placed in a niche half-way up the tower. Initially, its effect was unsatisfactory because 'the bead moulding running round the tower and continued in the niche has the effect of a rope encircling the neck of the apparently suspended victim', but the offending moulding was at once removed.[31] Another Albert Memorial clock-tower with a drinking fountain at its base, designed by R.D. Gould, was put up in Barnstaple, Devon, in 1862.[32]

Clock-towers were particularly suitable as commemorative monuments because in an age before most people owned watches, they were bound to be looked at. In addition,

90

their necessary height made them imposing structures, and the lower part of the tower could carry commemorative decoration. The design for the Belfast Albert Memorial clock-tower, by W.J. Barre (Plate 89), was selected after an architectural competition more fraught than most with intrigue and deception. The first design chosen, by the Belfast firm of Lanyon, Lynn and Lanyon (the firm of which the committee chairman was a member), was rejected in favour of Barre's when he guaranteed to have the tower built for £1,800 —the precise sum available. After Barre's death it was disclosed, in a law suit against his executors, that he had entered into a private agreement with the contractors, Thomas and William Fitzpatrick, who had told him that it could not be put up for much less than £4,000, to make an extra payment to them privately. The Belfast Albert Memorial clock-tower was completed in 1869. Like that at Hastings, it carries a niche with a statue of Prince Albert, in this case by S.F. Lynn.[33]

Although several Albert Memorials included drinking-fountains, the erection of just a drinking-fountain was more often considered too mean a gesture with which to honour the Prince Consort—and the proposal to erect an 'Albert Pump' in Faversham was described as 'pre-eminently ridiculous'.[34] However, a drinking-fountain by G.E. Street was put up in memory of the Prince at Chatham in 1863, in front of the schools which the architect had designed in 1860.[35] One type of imposing monumental structure was extremely convenient for the incorporation of a drinking-fountain. This was the Eleanor Cross, the suitability of which as a form for monuments to the Prince Consort had been so widely remarked.

The Albert Memorial at Queensbury, West Yorkshire (Plate 90), designed by Eli Milnes, stands outside Black Dyke Mills, and was presented by the mill owners, John Foster and

89. William Barre: Albert Memorial clock-tower, Belfast.

90. Eli Milnes: Albert Memorial drinking fountain, Queensbury.

Son, in 1863. It follows the pattern of the Eleanor Crosses, and has a drinking-fountain at its base. In the middle storey are four niches containing female allegorical figures representing Agriculture, Industry, Literature and the Fine Arts who rests her hand on a bust, presumably intended to represent the Prince Consort.[36] This ambitious monument is one of the most successful Albert memorials, effectively combining an ornamental and a practical function. It was also, of course, an effective advertisement for Foster and Son. Promoters of such monuments were criticised for 'trading on Prince Albert's name',[37] and though it is not clear whether Foster and Son increased their sales, some businessmen certainly did profit by the Prince Consort's death.

Clothiers began to advertise appropriate garments immediately after the announcements on 16 December from the Lord Chamberlain's Office informing those attending court what dress should be worn, and from the College of Arms instructing all other persons forthwith to 'put themselves into decent mourning' (Plate 91).[38] The demand for mourning was reported to be 'universal, far beyond precedent'.[39] Sir William Hardman observed that 'nothing is seen in all drapers', milliners', tailors', and haberdashers' shops but black',[40] while Elizabeth Gaskell commented that 'People could not give their orders at Lewis' and Allonbys for crying.'[41] The head of one of the largest drapery establishments in London was quoted as saying that even 'the poor people are coming in crowds to buy mourning' and that they 'will be satisfied with nothing but the best'.[42] Nevertheless, the demand led to the introduction of a cheaper material (a mixture of cotton and silk rather than pure silk) which became known as 'Albert crape'. The magazine *The Queen*, in its description of some of the mourning outfits available, also noted that pocket handkerchiefs 'with black borders' were in the shops, and although the writer doubted whether these would be used 'by the general public', a pattern for one with the words 'Albert Treu und Fest' for the reader to embroider was included (Plate 92).[43]

Black fabrics were also in demand for the draping of premises, furniture and objects, which was extensively practised. Commentators noted that 'even brass door plates' were covered with crape,[44] and observed 'the bows of black ribbon on the whips of the omnibus-drivers, and the black crape and ribbons on the badges of the conductors' in London on the day of the funeral.[45] Ribbons, such as those produced by the manufacturer Henry Slingsby of black and purple silk bands with the words 'IN MEMORY OF PRINCE ALBERT' woven in narrow stripes,[46] were also worn. It was presumably ribbons of this type

91. Children of the Orphan Working School making up their mourning for the Prince Consort, from *The Queen*, 4 January 1862.

92. Pattern for handkerchief embroidery, from *The Queen*, 28 December 1861.

93. (*far left*) Dalton and Barton: Silk bookmark, Victoria and Albert Museum.

94. Thomas Stevens: Silk picture of Prince Albert and his daughters. Victoria and Albert Museum.

which Princess Louise noticed the workpeople wearing in their buttonholes when she visited Wolverhampton with Queen Victoria in 1866 to unveil the statue of the Prince Consort there,[47] and which Flora Thompson records that her mother (who was only a child at the time) had worn, together with a black sash, while 'every lady in the land had gone into mourning'.[48]

The ribbon weavers of Coventry also seized the opportunity afforded by Prince Albert's death to promote their new venture into the field of woven pictures. The firms of Dalton and Barton, J. & J. Cash, and John Caldicott all produced woven silk portraits of the deceased Prince which were intended to be used as bookmarks (Plate 93). Larger examples, such as the one by Thomas Stevens dated 1863 showing Prince Albert surrounded by his five daughters (Plate 94), were mounted as pictures.[49]

Most of these silk portraits were based on photographs of the Prince taken during his lifetime. These too became commercial propositions after Prince Albert's death. Vernon Heath, for example, secured Queen Victoria's permission to sell copies of four different photographs of the Prince which were reported to have been the last portraits he sat for and which one commentator therefore thought would be 'the most satisfactory and the most gratifying acquisitions that can be obtained by the hundreds of thousands who love and honour the memory of the GOOD PRINCE'.[50] The demand for photographs was intense. It was reported that seventy thousand *carte-de-visite* size photographs (Plate 95) were sold within a week of Prince Albert's death,[51] and even in Paris one shopkeeper was said to have 'disposed of no less than 30,000' photographs.[52] This demand sometimes led to unscrupulous profiteering. The editor of *The Queen* was so inundated after the Prince's

95. Memorial *carte-de-visite* photograph of Prince Albert. National Portrait Gallery Archive, London.

96. (*far right*) Memorial print based on a photograph of Prince Albert by Messrs. Day. National Portrait Gallery Archive, London.

97. (*facing page*) La Port (pseud.): *The Last Moments of the late Prince Consort,* Wellcome Institute for the History of Medicine.

death with requests for copies of the photograph by Mayall which had been given away free with the issue of 2 November 1861, that he decided to secure further examples. These were now offered to readers (together with the companion photograph of the Queen) for 1s. with a copy of the magazine, or for 18d. on their own, by post or through booksellers.[53] The writer Arthur Munby recorded his own expensive endeavours to obtain a photograph: 'Crowds round the photograph shops, looking at the few portraits of the Prince which are still unsold. I went into Meclin's to buy one: every one in the shop was doing the same. They had none left: would put my name down, but could not promise even then. Afterwards I succeeded in getting one—the last the seller had—of the Queen and Prince: giving four shillings for what would have cost but eighteen pence a week ago.'[54]

Photographs by Mayall, Rejlander and others of the Prince during his lifetime were also used as the basis for many of the portraits which appeared in the press after his death, and for the numerous prints which were published. One of the most popular engravings, of which various versions exist, was based on a photograph taken at Osborne in 1861 by Messrs. Day (Plate 96). This print was originally intended for private circulation among members of the royal family, but Queen Victoria later gave her consent to its publication. *The Art Journal* described the engraving as 'unquestionably the best memorial the Queen's loving and loyal subjects can possess of one whose loss the nation still deplores'.[55]

Prints were also published after earlier paintings of the Prince. A profile head based on a miniature by W.C. Ross was engraved by William Holl and published by Smith, Elder and Co. in 1867, and Francis Holl engraved Landseer's crayon drawing of 1843 showing the seated Prince holding the Princess Royal in his arms, which was published in 1865. Queen Victoria herself gave prints after John Phillip's painting of Prince Albert in Highland Dress to the tenants of the Balmoral estate,[56] but a scheme to capitalise on his death by the

94

publication of lithographs after a picture entitled *The Last Moments of the late Prince Consort* (Plate 97), executed by an artist named Oakley under the pseudonym of La Port, met with strong royal disapproval.

Deathbed scenes formed the subject of many paintings and church monuments in the nineteenth century when such images were regarded as edifying for the onlooker. Indeed, a photograph of Oakley's painting inspired Robert Awde to compose a poem of the scene so that others might 'learn of Albert how a Prince should die!'[57]

Accounts of Prince Albert's last moments were included in most of the popular biographies, and one separate pamphlet on the subject was published.[58] The Queen and her family, however, presumably wished the scene to remain private, for only the barest facts had been given to the press, and there was evidently some concern in the royal household as to how the painter had managed to show the interior of the room. Nevertheless, it was known who had been present, but, oddly, the persons depicted around the bedside in Oakley's painting do not entirely correspond to official published accounts.[59]

There was considerable dismay that the 'horrible picture' was not 'dead & buried' when it was announced in February 1867 that it was to be exhibited at 222 Piccadilly (alongside William Holyoake's painting of the marriage of the Prince and Princess of Wales, and 'a life-size Venus') prior to being lithographed. After some discreet enquiries had been made, and various courses of action considered (including one to persuade an intermediary to purchase the painting and then destroy it), it was decided that the scheme would not succeed and no measures needed to be taken.[60] However, the painting was lithographed by W.L. Watson and the prints were published by C.J. Culliford. Coloured copies were sold for £1 1s. each under the auspices of the Art Union early in 1869. The purchasers also secured a stake in the lottery of the painting itself (valued at one thousand guineas) and other prizes.[61] The painting is now in the Wellcome Institute for the History of Medicine.

The Queen clearly did not approve of all the commercially-produced memorial images of Prince Albert. She also had reservations about utilitarian monuments, and her personal dislike of commemorative wares of a useful nature may explain the relative lack of these compared with the vast quantities of such items produced after the deaths of Nelson, Wellington and, especially, Princess Charlotte to whose unexpected and tragic end many commentators likened that of the Prince Consort.[62] The International Exhibition of 1862, in the planning of which Prince Albert had played a prominent role, and which might have acted as a shop window for merchandise of this type, showed only a few examples.[63] It is likely that most manufacturers, feeling genuine sympathy for their widowed sovereign, were unwilling to offend her by producing—for example—black transfer-printed 'Albert' mugs for tea and cocoa.

Nevertheless, a few ceramic objects commemorating the Prince Consort were manufactured. The Old Hall Pottery produced a jug with a medallion portrait of the Prince encircled by a wreath and with an elaborate handle composed of some of his orders and decorations (Plate 98).[64] The jug was displayed at the 1862 Exhibition where the Art Union of London showed a tazza designed by John Leighton and made by Copeland (Plate 99). This has a portrait of Prince Albert in the centre and panels commemorating his achievements in the fields of art, science and education. One hundred copies were given away as Art Union prizes in 1863.[65] A green transfer-printed jug showing the Prince in front of the Crystal Palace on one side, and with the 1862 Exhibition building in the background on

98. Jug commemorating the Prince Consort made by the Old Hall Pottery. Hereford and Worcester County Museum.

99. John Leighton: Tazza commemorating Prince Albert, made by Copeland. Victoria and Albert Museum.

100. George Abbott: Parian figure of Prince Albert, made by Copeland. Spode Limited Museum Collection.

the other, was also produced, but only one commemorative plate, with a half-length figure of Prince Albert, is known.[66] In the autumn of 1862, Copeland issued a seated statuette of the Prince in parian ware, modelled by George Abbott, which *The Art Journal* considered 'good as a likeness, and graceful as a figure' (Plate 100).[67]

A number of Birmingham firms registered designs for metalwork objects ranging from dress accessories, such as a brace buckle front[68] and a belt clasp (Plate 101),[69] to a pencil case with a bust of Prince Albert on top,[70] and a lamp with a portrait (Plate 102),[71] while a Rotherham company produced a design for an elaborate cast-iron hallstand surmounted by a medallion of the Prince flanked by two putti.[72] A tape measure with a photograph of Prince Albert (Plate 103) is in the Museum of London where there are also two commemorative medals. One by Ottley of Birmingham has a profile of the Prince on the obverse and the Lion of England with a figure of Britannia mourning over a sarcophagus on the reverse (Plate 104). The other medal, by Charles Weiner of Brussels, honours Prince Albert as the 'Founder of the International Exhibitions of 1851 and 1862'.[73]

Commemorative stationery, especially memorial cards (Plate 105), was also sold, and early in 1862 Messrs. Winsor and Newton issued an outline *In Memoriam* picture with armorial insignia of the Prince, a Union Jack at half-mast and other appropriate devices for 'amateur illuminators' to colour.[74] Popular biographies, some costing as little as one penny (Plate 106), began to appear within days of Prince Albert's death. Compiled largely from contemporary newspaper accounts, most of these concentrated on the Prince's last illness, death and funeral, and gave only a brief résumé of his life. Others, such as Reverend J.H. Wilson's *The Late Prince Consort: Reminiscences of his Life and Character*, sought to portray him as an exemplary Christian. By 1876, when a sixth edition (revised 'for elementary

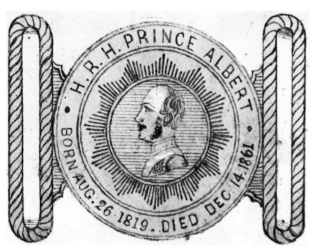

101. Design for a belt clasp. Public Record Office, London.

102. Design for a lamp. Public Record Office, London.

103. Tape measure with a photograph of Prince Albert. Museum of London.

104. Commemorative medal by Ottley of Birmingham. Museum of London.

In Memory of

HIS ROYAL HIGHNESS

The Prince Consort

OF

HER MOST GRACIOUS MAJESTY QUEEN VICTORIA,

Born August 26th, 1819,

Died December, 14th, 1861.

An illustrious Prince,—a wise Counsellor,—a loving Husband,—an affectionate Father.

Printed and Sold by J. H. Woodley, 30, Fore Street, City.

IN MEMORY OF

HIS ROYAL HIGHNESS

The Prince Consort

OF HER MOST GRACIOUS MAJESTY QUEEN VICTORIA,

BORN AUG. 26, 1819,—DIED DEC. 14, 1861.

Mysterious are the ways of God !
  Man cannot fathom them; nor know
Wherefore he now inflicts the rod,
  Or suffers sorrow here below.

Nations before him rise and fall :
  He overturneth whom he will.
The lowly rise up at His call,
  And some the highest places fill.

He taketh whom He will away;
  No hand can stay His mighty power.
The wisest, noblest, here to day
  May sink and die in one short hour.

Our nation mourns ! Long will it mourn
  For ALBERT, Consort of our Queen !
Death has been here—and, ruthless, torn
  Away an oak—all fresh and green.

Millions of hearts in sadness bow;
  Millions of knees all humbly bend ;
A nation mourns ; and men feel now
  That they have lost a dearest friend.

A nation mourns ! with her they mourn,
  Now widowed Queen of Queens the best !
God comfort her ! all lone, forlorn !
  God give her comfort, sweetest, best !

Almighty, hear us ! whilst we pray ;
  Look down upon this mournful scene ;
Our widowed Queen's deep sorrow stay !
  A nation prays, " God save the Queen."

                    JOSEPH SOUL.
ISLINGTON.

Woodley's Funeral Tablet Office, 30, Fore Street, City, London.

105. Memorial cards, printed by J.H. Woodley. British Library.

Reprinted from the "TELEGRAPH" and "TIMES."

MEMOIR

OF HIS LATE R.H.

PRINCE ALBERT.

Birth.	Devotion and Resignation of the Royal
Early Childhood.	Family.
Education.	Description of Coffins and Shell.
First Visit to England.	Public manifestations of grief.
Marriage.	Addresses of Condolence.
Public and Private Life.	The Funeral
His Last Hours and Death.	Appointments held by the Prince.

DIPROSE AND **PRICE ONE PENNY.** BATEMAN.

In Memoriam,

His Royal Highness the Prince Consort,

Elegy for the Pianoforte,

By

BRINLEY RICHARDS.

I KNOW THAT MY REDEEMER LIVETH

COPYRIGHT.

LONDON, ROBERT COCKS & Co NEW BURLINGTON STREET. W.
PUBLISHERS (BY SPECIAL WARRANT) TO HER MOST GRACIOUS MAJESTY.

106. Title page from a popular memoir of Prince Albert. British Library.

107. Cover for music composed in memory of Prince Albert. British Library.

schools') was brought out, 20,000 copies had been sold. A weightier tome, *Prince Albert's Golden Precepts*, was published in the spring of 1862 at 2s. 6d. The Crown Princess of Prussia commented that she was 'so glad' that some of her father's 'sublime maxims and principles should be brought before the British public in a popular form',[75] but a reviewer in *The Athenaeum* regretted that the context of these sayings was not recorded.[76]

An ambitious work by William Thomas Kime, entitled *Albert the Good: A nation's tribute of affection to the memory of a truly virtuous Prince*, was published in the summer of 1862. This book, illustrated with portraits of the Prince, was a compilation of articles and obituaries which had appeared in national, provincial and foreign newspapers, and weekly and monthly journals; of sermons and addresses delivered on the occasion of his death; and of memorial poems, hymns and ballads which had appeared in the press or as separate publications. The last section of the book contains 'Material towards a biography of the Prince', presumably for amateur authors to fill in!

Kime's book prints memorial ballads and hymns, including A.B. McLuckie's *Affection's Wreath of Flowers*. Set to music and published by J.H. Jewell, this was inspired by a report that, prior to the coffin being closed, a wreath of flowers made by Princess Alice was placed

100

on Prince Albert's body. Other memorial music was published. Robert Cocks and Company offered an elegy for piano entitled *In Memoriam His Late Royal Highness the Prince Consort* by Brinley Richards for 3 shillings (Plate 107). Sympathy for the bereaved monarch was also expressed in music, for example in W.S. Passmore's *God Bless Our Loved Queen*, set to music by W.T. Wrighton, and *Our Widowed Queen* by F.A. Lewis with music by Dr. A.S. Holloway. The Reverend Newman Hall adapted the words of the National Anthem for the occasion. .

The tone of many of these memorial tributes reflects the sympathy which was genuinely felt by the public for the bereaved Queen. For example, upon hearing of the Prince Consort's death, Charles Dickens postponed some readings he was due to give at Liverpool because, as he told W.H. Wills, his sub-editor, 'I feel personally that the Queen has always been very considerate and gracious to me, and I would on no account do anything that might seem unfeeling or disrespectful.'[77] Only one month later, however, observing the general hysteria, Dickens was disrespectful enough to comment upon 'the Jackasses that people are at present making of themselves . . .!'[78] Such extravagant public expressions of sympathy could not last long, and, indeed, feelings of pity also began to wane as Queen Victoria failed to return to normal life after the accepted period of mourning was over.

The Queen did not appear in public after her bereavement until 13 October 1863 when she unveiled the statue of Prince Albert at Aberdeen (Plate 108). For this ceremony the local inhabitants were instructed to refrain from cheering, employing bands of music, and

108. Unveiling of the statue of Prince Albert at Aberdeen, from *The Illustrated London News*, 24 October 1863.

from decorating their houses and the streets with the usual banners, triumphal arches, and flowers of such occasions.[79] The teeming rain in which the unveiling was conducted was seen as peculiarly appropriate for a ceremony which was more 'funeral than festive'.[80] The Queen afterwards acknowledged the 'consideration' shown to her by the people on this 'sad & trying & painful' occasion.[81] *The Times*, however, remonstrated that two years was long enough to spend 'in unavailing regrets and in dwelling upon days which cannot be recalled'.[82] To her subjects it increasingly seemed as if their sovereign had lost all interest in life, and was concerned exclusively with the commemoration of the dead, for during the 1860s she was rarely seen in public except to unveil statues of the Prince Consort. In 1864 she presided over the inauguration at Perth, which she described as 'very trying very *very* overpowering',[83] and the following year she travelled to Coburg with all her children to attend the unveiling of Theed's statue (Plate 68). She observed that this was 'the most beautiful, touching & solemn Ceremony' she ever saw,[84] but the occasion was also used to chastise her for her continued seclusion. *The Times* commented:

> Nothing can be more simple and natural than such a proceeding, and nothing is on the first impulse more calculated to awaken sympathetic respect. Only when we remember the years which have passed between the death of the Prince and the inauguration of his statue, only when we call to mind the repeated monuments in all places associated with his memory, only when we think of a prolonged seclusion, do we feel the danger of indulging in the luxury of sorrow.[85]

Certainly, by this time, monuments seemed to be appearing everywhere: 'If you should meet with an inaccessible cave anywhere', wrote Dickens to his friend and illustrator, John Leech, in September 1864, 'to which a hermit could retire from the memory of Prince Albert and testimonials to the same, pray let me know of it. We have nothing solitary and deep enough in this part of England.'[86] It was suggested that Prince Albert's most conspicuous attribute had been his devotion to duty, and that while 'costly marbles and sumptuous monuments are good, and their dedication to memorial service is laudable . . . it would be an indifferent mode of showing respect for such a man to accumulate monuments to his honour, and to neglect the example of his life . . . the deepest respect which can be paid to the virtues of the Prince Consort is to strive to practise them in all the relations of Social and Royal life'.[87]

The Queen's behaviour also gave rise to criticism because she sought also to deprive the public of the junketing normally associated with the celebration of happier royal events. Nobody had minded that Princess Alice's wedding in July 1862 had been a quiet family affair at Osborne (described by the Queen herself as 'more like a funeral than a wedding', with 'everyone steeped in mourning'),[88] but the marriage of the Prince of Wales the following year was quite another matter. The melancholy spectacle of yet another inauguration ceremony was no substitute for the great public celebrations which were expected on the occasion of the marriage of the heir to the throne. Queen Victoria, however, strove 'to deprive the entrance of the Princess of Wales into London of almost all pomp & significance'[89] because of 'the court mourning for the Prince Consort'.[90] The equipage which she selected for the procession was so shabby that the press felt bound to comment. Tactfully, nothing was said publicly about the reason for this, but as one shrewd observer noted privately 'no secret is made by those about the Court. H.M. has not been wise in this respect'. He went on to note that the Queen 'compared the reception given to the Princess with that offered to her late husband—as if any comparison could be fairly made'.[91] A wedding-day family portrait by Mayall (Plate 109) shows the Queen contemplating Theed's bust of Prince Albert, studiously ignoring the Prince and Princess of Wales standing behind in all their finery. The Queen did not attend the wedding breakfast, and, dressed in widow's weeds, she watched the wedding ceremony in St. George's Chapel in front of 'the beautiful window, altar and reredos to my beloved one's memory' from a gallery, only mastering her emotions 'by a violent effort'. She was later 'soothed and calmed' by a visit to the Mausoleum, and a prayer 'by that beloved resting-place'.[92] Nonetheless, thousands of people turned out to watch the wedding procession, and the occasion prompted the production of quantities of commemorative items.

As the years went by, the Queen's continued retirement from public life had more serious political consequences, providing fuel for the emerging republican movement. In 1871 Charles Wentworth Dilke, a Radical Member of Parliament, openly challenged the concept of monarchy, arguing that it was an expensive anachronism, and criticising Queen Victoria for her dereliction of duty. At the same time a pamphlet entitled *What Does She Do With It?* was circulating, in which the author, 'Solomon Temple, Builder' (actually a Liberal M.P., George Otto Trevelyan) claimed that the Queen was hoarding vast sums of public money voted for the purpose of royal ceremonial. The pamphlet was widely read, and provoked considerable debate.[93]

By the late autumn of 1871, the republican movement seemed to be gaining ground, and it is possible that the British monarchy was saved by what could have been a catastrophe—the reappearance of typhoid fever in the royal family. In November the Prince of Wales fell ill and, as the tenth anniversary of his father's death approached, his life, too, appeared to be in danger. Public criticism of the Queen changed into sympathy for her as she anxiously waited. On the fatal anniversary, the Prince of Wales began to recover. There was general rejoicing, and support for Dilke withered in the face of it. Queen Victoria's cousin, the Duke of Cambridge, wrote to his mother, with a great sense of relief:

109. Queen Victoria with the Prince and Princess of Wales and a bust of Prince Albert, March 1863.

'The Republicans say their chances are up—Thank God for this! Heaven has sent this dispensation to save us.'[94]

A public service of Thanksgiving for the Prince's recovery was held in St. Paul's Cathedral on 27 February 1872. It was a tremendous success. The Queen, who had somewhat reluctantly agreed to the event on the condition that it was to be conducted without any 'ostentatious pomp', noted afterwards 'the millions out, the beautiful decorations, the wonderful enthusiasm and astounding affectionate loyalty shown'.[95]

Though the future of the royal family was once again secure, their popularity was not yet completely re-established. The Queen was still rarely to be seen in public and murmurings against her continued to be heard from time to time. Until the 1880s, as Flora Thompson recalls, most ordinary people took 'little interest in the Royal House. The Queen and the Prince and Princess of Wales were sometimes mentioned, but with little respect and no affection. "The Old Queen" as she was called, was supposed to have shut herself up in Balmoral Castle with a favourite servant named John Brown and to have refused to open Parliament when Mr. Gladstone begged her to.'

As 1887 approached, however, 'a new spirit was abroad . . . The Queen, it appeared, had reigned fifty years. She had been a good queen, a wonderful queen . . . the tradesmen gave lovely coloured portraits of her in her crown and garter ribbon on their almanacks, most of which were framed at home and hung up in the cottages. Jam could be bought in glass jugs adorned with her profile in hobnails and inscribed "1837 to 1887. Victoria the Good".'[96] Vast quantities of commemorative wares of this type were produced, and some of these items incorporated portraits of Prince Albert.

Queen Victoria's Golden Jubilee was celebrated in towns throughout the British Isles and Empire, but among many events, the focus was the procession and Thanksgiving Service in Westminster Abbey on 22 June, watched by multitudes. Although the Queen at first viewed the celebrations without enthusiasm, the display of public loyalty and affection encouraged her to abandon forever her former seclusion. The year 1887 finally saw her return to a full public life, and prominent among the many tributes which the Jubilee inspired, was to be a gift from the Women of Great Britain and the British Empire, paid for by a fund composed of subscriptions ranging from one penny to one pound. The Queen intimated that a replica of Marochetti's equestrian figure of Prince Albert erected twenty years earlier at Glasgow (Plate 66) 'found most favour in her eyes',[97] as the gift but her choice caused some disquiet. Knollys wrote to Ponsonby on 9 December 1886:

> I am quite sure the Prince of Wales would be the last person in the world to wish to hurt the Queen's feelings about a Statue of the Prince Consort—He only thinks that to erect a Statue of one who will have been dead for 25 years is not quite an appropriate memorial for the purpose of celebrating a joyful event in the life of a living Person . . . I don't think you hear these things (naturally so) as much as I do but I am afraid (& I hope you will not mind my mentioning it) People have had almost enough of the Prince Consort, and another Statue of him would provoke remarks which if the Queen knew they were made would pain her.[98]

These views were shared by the members of the committee who were convinced that if it became known that the funds were to be used 'to perpetuate once more the likeness of a

110. Unveiling of J.E. Boehm's statue of Prince Albert in Windsor Great Park, from *The Illustrated London News*, 17 May 1890.

Prince whom so many have forgotten & so many more never saw', they would have 'no more chance of obtaining money for it, than of getting the moon out of the sky'.[99] Indeed, when news of the form of the proposed monument (which the committee attempted to keep quiet) was leaked to the press, subscriptions promptly came to a halt. They did not revive until the Queen consented to any surplus monies being devoted to a charitable object, and then subscriptions flooded in—£75,000 was raised for the Queen Victoria Jubilee Institute for Nurses in addition to the £10,000 for the statue. This work, by J.E. Boehm, was unveiled in Windsor Great Park on 12 May 1890 (Plate 110).[100]

Although a few statues and other images of Prince Albert were put up after this date,[101] these were invariably in conjunction with monuments to Queen Victoria, and should be seen as part of the general expression of loyalty to the throne. The public cult of the Prince Consort, which had manifested itself in extravagant displays of mourning, and in an unprecedented number of memorial schemes, had gradually faded away. After 1887, if there were any cult figure, then it was Queen Victoria herself, and the public testified their devotion to her in hundreds of tributes and monuments. Although she had supplanted Prince Albert in the public consciousness, her own worship of her husband's memory lasted until she died in 1901. The Queen outlived most of her contemporaries, and a new generation had grown up who knew no more than that the Prince Consort 'had been the Queen's husband, though, oddly enough, not the King, and that he had been so good that nobody had liked him in his lifetime, excepting the Queen, who "fairly doted"'.[102] For most Edwardians, Prince Albert was ancient history.

Notes

INTRODUCTION
Documents in the Royal Archives are prefixed by the letters RA.

1. British Library, Add. MS. 43764, Diary of Lord Broughton, xxi, 1861-2, f.106 v.
2. The shock was all the greater because no official bulletins on the Prince's state of health were issued until the last week of his life—and these remained optimistic until the day before he died. See W. Schupbach, 'The Last Moments of H.R.H. the Prince Consort', *Medical History*, xxvi, 1982, pp. 321-4.
3. As note 1.
4. Thomas Carlyle, *On Heroes, Hero-Worship and the Heroic in History*, London, 1840.
5. *Ibid.*, p. 10.
6. British Library, Add. MS. 43764, f. 110.
7. S.M.Ellis (ed.), *A mid-Victorian Pepys: The Letters and Memoirs of Sir William Hardman, M.A., F.R.G.S.*, London, 1923, p. 70.
8. *Illustrated Weekly News*, 28 December 1861, p. 180.
9. J. A. V. Chapple and Arthur Pollard (eds.), *The Letters of Mrs. Gaskell*, Manchester, 1966, p. 496.
10. Theodore Martin, *The Life of His Royal Highness the Prince Consort*, 5 vols., London, 1875-80, ii, p. 537.
11. For a full account of this memorial see *The Survey of London*, London, 1900 onwards, xxxviii, *The Museums Area of South Kensington and Westminster*, 1975 (hereafter referred to as *Survey of London*), chapter viii.

NOTES TO CHAPTER ONE

1. C. Woodham-Smith, *Queen Victoria: Her Life and Times 1819-1861*, London, 1972, pp. 504-5.
2. R. Fulford (ed.), *Dearest Mama: Letters between Queen Victoria and the Crown Princess of Prussia 1861-1864*, London 1968 (hereafter referred to as *Dearest Mama*), p. 24.
3. Queen Victoria to Herr Florschütz, 3 January 1862, quoted in H. Bolitho (ed.), *The Prince Consort and his brother*, London, 1933, p. 219.
4. A. C. Benson and Viscount Esher (eds.), *The Letters of Queen Victoria*, first series, 3 vols., London, 1908, iii, Queen Victoria to the King of the Belgians, 20 December 1861.
5. As note 3.
6. *Dearest Mama*, p. 47.
7. As note 3.
8. Geoffrey Rowell, *Hell and the Victorians*, Oxford, 1974, p. 9.
9. Macleod contributed a paper entitled 'Social Life in Heaven' to a symposium on 'The Recognition of Friends in Heaven' in 1866, which was published under that title in the same year.
10. W. Branks, *Heaven our Home*, Edinburgh, 1861, pp. 273-4.

11. *The Last Hours of His Royal Highness Prince Albert, of Blessed Memory*, London, 1864 (reprinted from *The Northern Whig*).
12. British Library, Add. MSS. 62089 and 62090.
13. Charles Tennyson, *Alfred Tennyson*, London, 1949, p. 336.
14. Hope Dyson and Charles Tennyson (eds.), *Dear and Honoured Lady: The Correspondence between Queen Victoria and Alfred Tennyson*, London, 1969, p. 67.
15. *Ibid.*, p. 69.
16. Charles Tennyson, *op. cit.*, pp. 335-6; Dyson and Tennyson, *op. cit.*, pp. 60-7. The Dedication was incorporated into a new edition of the *Idylls of the King* which was being printed at the time of Prince Albert's death. Queen Victoria asked, however, that several copies of it should be printed separately.
17. *Dearest Mama*, p. 47.
18. Colonel the Hon. F. A. Wellesley (ed.), *The Paris Embassy during the Second Empire: Selections from the Papers of Henry Richard Charles Wellesley, 1st Earl Cowley, Ambassador at Paris 1852-1867*, London, 1928, p. 242.
19. Arnold Florance, *Queen Victoria at Osborne*, Newport, Isle of Wight, 1977, p. 29.
20. Theed is reported to have said on his return from Windsor that Prince Albert's face 'was peaceful, all but lines of suffering about the mouth', C.E. Smith (ed.), *Journals and Correspondence of Lady Eastlake*, 2 vols., London, 1895, ii, p. 164.
21. *Dearest Mama*, p. 45. Queen Victoria and Prince Albert had had casts made of the arms and legs of some of their children when they were babies: these are now at Osborne.
22. *Ibid.*, p. 28.
23. *Ibid.*, p. 28.
24. *Ibid.*, p. 46.
25. RA Z12/64.
26. RA Z12/71.
27. *Dearest Mama*, p. 24.
28. D. Bennett, *King without a Crown*, London, 1977, p. 376.
29. RA Add. U/32, 27 January 1862.
30. RA Add. U/32, 23 December 1861. A memorandum from the Lord Chamberlain's Office, dated 25 March 1862, stated that 'the Blue Room at Windsor Castle . . . should remain in the present state and shall not be made use of in the future'. Vera Watson, *A Queen at Home*, London, 1952, p. 156. The Crown Princess assisted her mother in the decoration of 'the sad but sacred room', sending, for example, 'a very fine china picture of the "Madonna del Candelabre" which dearest Papa was so fond of', and later painting a picture of an angel. *Dearest Mama*, pp. 31, 32, 156.
31. *Dearest Mama*, pp. 154-5.
32. RA PP2/80/6668.
33. Queen Victoria wrote to Princess Alice on 13 February 1864: 'the beautiful Pedestal for darling Papa's Bust is placed in the *Hall* & is unique in its way. It was placed on the dearest 10th.' RA Add. U/143. As with several of Queen Victoria's memorials to her husband, significant dates were chosen for their inauguration: February 10th was the date of their wedding.
34. *The Private Life of the Queen*, 1897, reprinted, Old Woking, 1979, p. 201.
35. Queen Victoria had wished Winterhalter to execute this portrait, but the painter refused to come to England because of his poor health. Albert Graefle was her second choice: she

observed to the Crown Princess, 'I think after Winterhalter his likenesses are far the best.' *Dearest Mama*, p. 209.

36. RA Queen Victoria's Journal, 25 February 1863. This entry suggests that the picture was originally to have shown Queen Victoria, Princess Alice and the three youngest children only.

37. RA Add. U/143, 25 June 1863.

38. RA Add. U/143, 16 December 1863. See also M.H. Noel-Paton, *Tales of a Grand-daughter*, Elgin, Moray, 1970, pp. 34-5.

39. M.H. Noel-Paton, *op. cit.*, p. 34.

40. *Ibid.*, pp. 33, 36; D. and F. Irwin, *Scottish Painters at Home and Abroad 1700-1900*, London, 1975, pp. 318-19; *Art Journal*, 1895, p. 124. Paton exhibited the sketches of the heads of Queen Victoria, Princesses Helena, Louise, Beatrice and Alice at the Royal Scottish Academy in 1866, and some of them were acquired by the royal family after the painter's death. The painter George Richmond, who was summoned to Windsor soon after the Prince Consort's death to make a sketch of the corpse, also excused himself on the grounds of ill-health, although it is believed that he really found the prospect too morbid. Raymond Lister, *George Richmond: A critical biography*, London, 1981, p. 88.

41. W.E. Aytoun, *Lays of the Scottish Cavaliers*, Edinburgh and London, 1863. Paton recorded that during a sitting with the Princesses Beatrice and Louise on 26 November 1863, Lady Augusta Bruce (to whom he had given a copy of the book) 'ran in ... to say the Queen had been very much struck with the illustrations of *Lays of the Scottish Cavaliers* ... and had been wondering whether I could make for her a small design of her kneeling beside the bed on which the Prince Consort died. I went with Mrs. B. to the room, where I gave as well as I could, on the spur of the moment, my idea on the subject and the mode in which I thought it should be treated ...' M.H. Noel-Paton, *op. cit.*, p. 35.

42. RA Add. U/32, 30 March 1864. The painting is now lost.

43. D. and F. Irwin, *op. cit.*, p. 322. The similarity between the painting and Theed's statue was noted by *The Illustrated London News*, 2 November 1867, p. 481. Phillip's painting seems to have been considered a suitable model for public statues of the Prince Consort. One proposal for the Albert memorial at Perth was for a Prince Albert Literary Institute, School of Art and Design, and Museum, in which a statue of the Prince Consort after Phillip's portrait would be placed (*Perthshire Courier*, 7 July 1863). At Aberdeen, in consequence of some dissatisfaction with Marochetti's figure of the Prince when it was unveiled in 1863, a second memorial statue by William Brodie was proposed, which was to be based on Phillip's painting (*Aberdeen Herald*, 17 October 1863, p. 8). Neither proposal was carried out.

44. R. Fulford (ed.), *Your Dear Letter: Private Correspondence of Queen Victoria and the Crown Princess of Prussia 1865-1871*, London, 1971, p. 125.

45. RA Queen Victoria's Journal, 1 January 1862.

46. RA Queen Victoria's Journal, 8, 10 May 1862.

47. RA Queen Victoria's Journal, 15 August 1862.

48. RA Add. U/143, 26 August 1862.

49. RA PP2/63/4035, PP2/66/4466.

50. RA Queen Victoria's Journal, 17 October 1863.

51. The plaster model of the statue was exhibited at the Royal Academy in 1864, and is currently on loan to the Victoria and Albert Museum from the Royal Collection.

52. RA PP2/88/7934, PP2/97/9377.

53. RA Queen Victoria's Journal, 6 June 1864. This model was not wasted, but was cast and erected in the grounds of the Duchess of Sutherland's house at Cliveden, Buckinghamshire in 1866. Harriet Leveson-Gower, Duchess of Sutherland, was appointed Mistress of the Robes on Queen Victoria's accession, and became a firm friend of the Queen, and a great admirer of Prince Albert. She was taken into the Blue Room at Windsor to see the Prince Consort on his deathbed, and was one of the Queen's closest companions during the early weeks of her widowhood.

54. It was reported in *The Private Life of the Queen*. 1897, reprinted, Old Woking, 1979, p. 212-13, that every year on 26 August Queen Victoria, her family and court, servants and tenants gathered together at the foot of the statue and 'amid the most impressive silence, and with bared heads' drank to the memory of the dead. However, this account cannot be substantiated—indeed, on several occasions Queen Victoria was not at Balmoral at that date.

Bronze statuettes based on Theed's figure of Prince Albert in Highland dress were also produced by Elkington's. Queen Victoria presented one to the Duke of Cambridge (RA PP2/88/7934), and an example from the Royal Collection was shown at the exhibition '*This Brilliant Year*' Queen Victoria's Jubilee 1887, Royal Academy of Arts, 1977 (92).

55. E. Longford, *Victoria R.I.*, London, 1966, p. 386. Queen Victoria also planted an oak tree in Windsor Great Park to mark the spot where Prince Albert had had his last day's shooting. The ceremony, which took place on 25 November 1862, is recorded in photographs in the Royal Archives, in W. Menzies, *Windsor Great Park*, 1864, and *The Illustrated London News*, 20 December 1862, p. 645. It prompted the suggestion that on the first anniversary of Prince Albert's death, people should follow the Queen's example and plant an Albert oak, but it appears that few people did so.

56. *The Times*, 9 July 1863, p. 10. See also *Saturday Review*, 13 June 1863, pp. 756-7; *Perthshire Courier*, 14 July 1863. The lines of the inscription, which were adapted from the Wisdom of Solomon, Chapter 4, had been sent to the Queen by the Crown Princess, though perhaps not with this purpose in mind. *Dearest Mama*, pp. 101-2.

57. RA Queen Victoria's Journal, 19 March 1863.

58. RA Queen Victoria's Journal, 13 March 1865.

59. The group is now in the Royal Mausoleum at Frogmore. The plaster model was exhibited at the Royal Academy in 1868, and is now on loan from the Royal Collection to the National Portrait Gallery.

60. RA PP2/123/13137.

61. On 17 March 1862 Queen Victoria recorded visiting Theed's studio to see the sculptor's 'new sketch, for the group of us together, Vicky's idea, & in which she has helped him much. It is lovely.' (RA Queen Victoria's Journal, 17 March 1862). The Queen's use of the word 'new' suggests that an earlier, perhaps different, treatment had been abandoned.

62. On nineteenth-century enthusiasm for Anglo-Saxon subjects see Roy Strong, *And when did you last see your father? The Victorian Painter and British History*, London, 1978, pp. 114-18, 155-6.

63. On this aspect of royal taste see *Van Dyck in Check Trousers: Fancy Dress in Art and Life 1700-1900*, Scottish National Portrait Gallery, 1978, pp. 67-70.

64. As note 3.

65. *Dearest Mama*, p. 188.

66. *Ibid.*, p. 185.

67. RA Queen Victoria's Journal, 30 March 1863; *Dearest Mama*, p. 188.

68. *Dearest Mama*, p. 189.
69. RA Z15/7.
70. RA Z16/44.
71. RA Z17/16. The bust is now lost. The Crown Princess reported to the Queen in 1872 that she had commissioned a replica of Emil Wolff's bust of Prince Albert at Buckingham Palace, for her bedroom at Berlin, adding 'it does not do dear Papa justice but it is so sweet I think!', RA Z27/8.
72. *Dearest Mama*, p. 45. She also gave Prince Alfred and Princess Hohenlohe plaster casts after Theed's bust, for example. RA PP2/80/6668.
73. This was presented early this century to the 1st Battalion Kings Royal Rifle Corps by Prince and Princess Christian of Schleswig-Holstein in memory of their son who died at Pretoria in 1900 during the Boer War. It is now in the possession of the Royal Green Jackets.
74. Theodore Martin, *The Life of His Royal Highness the Prince Consort*, 5 vols., London, 1875–80, i, p. 212. Martin records that the Queen made this remark on 20 December 1873.
75. RA Y166/4, 15 May 1867.
76. RA Queen Victoria's Journal, 12 February 1864. Queen Victoria recorded in her journal for 19 January 1863 that the idea for this painting came from Corbould himself.
77. It would appear that Corbould originally proposed more than one crowning statuette, for in her journal for 16 February 1864 Queen Victoria observed that the artist had 'altered the one design chosen, as at my own particular request & desire *only* dearest Albert's statuette is to be brought in, taken from the beautiful allegorical picture in armour, sheathing his sword with the words "I have fought the good Fight". Louise has also been helping & shows great taste.'
78. The verse on the front panel reads:

    My Rose of love with tears I laid on earth;
    My Lily's purity hath soared to Heaven;
    But Faith still lives, and sees in this new birth,
    How both once more to cheer my soul are given.

    The verses on the other two panels are:

    Fight the good fight he fought, and still like him
    Cherish the flowers of Purity and love:
    So shall he, when thy earthly joys grow dim,
    First greet thee in our Saviour's home above.

    Walk as he walked in faith and righteousness;
    Strive as he strove, the weak and poor to aid.
    Seek not thyself but other men to bless;
    So win like him a wreath that will not fade.

79. RA Add. U/143, 20 February 1864.
80. On the imagery of these memorial works see also Mark Girouard, *The Return to Camelot: Chivalry and the English Gentleman*, New Haven and London, 1981, pp. 114–16, 125–6.
81. RA PP2/66/4466, PP2/66/4869, Queen Victoria's Journal, 19 December 1862. The bust given to Sir James Clark was shown at the exhibition 'This Brilliant Year' Queen Victoria's Jubilee 1887, Royal Academy of Arts, 1977, (91). The inscription on the back records that it was presented by the Queen on 25 December 1862. Sir Charles Phipps became Keeper of the Privy Purse to Queen Victoria in 1849.
82. Theodore Martin, *Queen Victoria As I Knew Her*, Edinburgh and London, 1908, p. 104.
83. *Dearest Mama*, pp. 219–20.
84. General Grey, *The Early Years of His Royal Highness the Prince Consort*, London, 1867, p. ix.
85. Queen Victoria, *Leaves from the Journal of Our Life in the Highlands, from 1848–1861*, London, 1868, preface.
86. E.A. Helps (ed.), *Correspondence of Sir Arthur Helps K.C.B., D.C.L.*, London, 1917, pp. 253–4.
87. RA Add. U/32, 14 December 1867.
88. RA Add. U/143, 24 November 1862.
89. *Dearest Mama*, p. 148. The 'holy days' were the 17th, 18th and 23rd December: the mausoleum was consecrated on the 17th, Prince Albert's coffin was placed within on the 18th, and the funeral took place on the 23rd.
90. *Ibid.*, p. 290.
91. RA Add. U/32, 27 January 1862.
92. British Library, Add. MSS. 43764, f. 120.
93. Vera Watson, *op. cit.*, p. 156.
94. Col. the Hon. F.A. Wellesley (ed.), *op. cit.*, p. 241.
95. *The Times*, 12 October 1863, p. 8.

NOTES TO CHAPTER TWO

1. *The Royal Mausoleum, Frogmore* (guidebook), Windsor, 1968, p. 2.
2. RA M10/72 and 73. W. Ames, *Prince Albert and Victorian Taste*, London, 1967, p. 111.
3. RA Y172/32.
4. C. Ruland, *The Works of Raphael ... as represented in the Raphael Collection in the Royal Library at Windsor Castle, formed by H.R.H. the Prince Consort 1853–1861 and completed by Her Majesty Queen Victoria*, London, 1876.
5. Many of Humbert's drawings for Whippingham Church and its Albert memorial survive at Osborne House, and the model for the monument is on loan from the Royal Collection to the Victoria and Albert Museum.
6. *Dearest Mama*, p. 32.
7. Theodore Martin, *The Life of His Royal Highness the Prince Consort*, 5 vols., London, 1875–80, v, p. 199.
8. *Dearest Mama*, p. 36.
9. The Queen lived another forty years by which time the whereabouts of her effigy had been forgotten. Lord Esher recalled in February 1901 that 'After a minute enquiry, an old workman remembered that about 1865 the figure had been walled up in the stores at Windsor. The brickwork was taken down, and the figure found. It is now over the tomb, a really impressive thing by Marochetti. It was pure chance that it was discovered.' *Journals and Letters of Reginald, Viscount Esher*, edited by M.V. Brett and Oliver, Viscount Esher, 4 vols., London 1934–8, i, p. 282.
10. RA PP Windsor 396.
11. RA PP Windsor 417.
12. RA PP Windsor 432.
13. RA PP Windsor 435. *Builder*, xxi, 1863, pp. 152–3.
14. RA PP Add. Vic 1598.
15. RA Queen Victoria's Journal, 15 March 1862.
16. RA R18/47-50.
17. *Dearest Mama*, pp. 137–8.
18. RA R18/8.
19. The plinth on which the sarcophagus was to rest eventually had to be made from five pieces of black Belgian marble which was presented for the purpose by Leopold I of the Belgians, although they did not arrive until after his death. RA PP Windsor 552, 560, 563, 611, 616.
20. RA Add. U/32, 23 December 1861.

21. RA R18/12.
22. RA Queen Victoria's Journal, 20 February 1862.
23. RA Add. U/143, 24 November 1862.
24. RA Queen Victoria's Journal, 17 December 1862.
25. RA Queen Victoria's Journal, 18 December 1862.
26. RA PP Windsor 427.
27. RA Queen Victoria's Journal, 19 December 1862.
28. RA R18/61.
29. RA PP Windsor 433.
30. RA PP Windsor 518.
31. RA PP Windsor 608, H.T. Harrison to Phipps, 31 January 1866. In May 1863 the possibility was explored of using Government gun-metal for some of the decorative castings by Barbedienne, but the Government refused to supply it. RA R18/437, 440.
32. RA PP Windsor 570, 572.
33. RA PP Windsor 550.
34. RA Queen Victoria's Journal, 28 November 1864.
35. RA Queen Victoria's Journal, 30 November 1864.
36. RA Queen Victoria's Journal, 26 November 1868. The full-size plaster model for the effigy of Prince Albert, and also for that of Queen Victoria, are on loan to the Victoria and Albert Museum from the Royal Collection. There are two plaster reductions of the effigy of Prince Albert at Osborne House.
37. RA Queen Victoria's Journal, 10 June 1864.
38. RA R18/83. No suitable Raphael composition could be found for the *Crucifixion* picture. The *Apotheosis* in the entrance chapel was painted by Frankl from a cartoon by the Crown Princess.
39. RA PP Windsor 571.
40. The mural decoration was carried out by the London firm of William Homann. The dome was originally painted deep blue and dotted with gold stars, but it was repainted with angels by Ion Pace in 1909 as a tribute to Queen Victoria by her son, then Edward VII. He also renewed all the glass originally designed by Grüner, and the ambulatory windows which carried figures of angels chosen by the Crown Princess from compositions by Fra. Angelico.
41. Theodore Martin, *The Life of his Royal Highness the Prince Consort*, 5 vols., London, 1875-80, v, p. 199.
42. W. Ames, *op. cit.*, p. 9. RA Queen Victoria's Journal, 31 August 1845.
43. RA R18/6.
44. RA R18/62.
45. RA PP Windsor 557.
46. 'Herne the Hunter' (pseud.), *A Fragment from the Fine Art Follies of Frogmore*, Windsor, 1869, p. 15.
47. *Ibid.*, pp. 7, 14.
48. *Dearest Mama*, p. 10.
49. RA PP Windsor 383A. The Dean repeated his idea in a letter to General Grey of 7 February 1862 (RA R40/1). For the early history of this chapel see W.H. St. John Hope, *Windsor Castle, an architectural history*, 3 vols., London, 1913, ii, pp. 478-89.
50. RA PP Windsor 383D, R40/1.
51. RA R40/1.
52. RA R40/1. The Prince's coffin lay in St. George's Chapel until 18 December 1862 when it was installed in the mausoleum.
53. RA R40/1.
54. RA PP Windsor 383E.
55. RA R40/6; Queen Victoria's Journal, 16 April 1862.
56. RA R40/8.

57. RA R40/9.
58. RA Queen Victoria's Journal, 26 May 1862.
59. RA Queen Victoria's Journal, 29 March 1862.
60. RA PP Windsor 468.
61. RA PP Windsor 473.
62. RA PP Windsor 469.
63. Theodore Martin, *The Life of his Royal Highness the Prince Consort*, 5 vols., London, 1875-80, iii, p. 346.
64. *Art Journal*, 1874, p. 368; J. and M. Davison, *The Triqueti Marbles in the Albert Memorial Chapel, Windsor: a series of photographs executed by the Misses Davison*, London, 1876, introduction. One of these panels was bought from the 1862 Exhibition by the South Kensington (now the Victoria and Albert) Museum.

    Triqueti had also lent Prince Albert two drawings by Raphael to be photographed for the volume he was compiling of all known works by the master. C.F. Bell, *Annals of Thomas Banks*, Cambridge, 1938, pp. 206-7.
65. RA PP Windsor 469a.
66. *Ibid.*
67. RA PP Windsor 469b.
68. Dorothy D. Bosomworth, *The Revival of Mosaic as a Technique of Wall Decoration in the second half of the Nineteenth Century*, (Paper presented at the Annual Conference of the Victorian Society, 1978), p. 10. Salviati had installed mosaics in the eastern end of Exeter College Chapel, Oxford in 1860.
69. RA PP Windsor 471.
70. RA PP Windsor 475.
71. Dorothy D. Bosomworth, *op. cit.*, pp. 8-9.
72. RA PP Windsor 527. Difficulties in obtaining from Coburg appropriate heraldry to be used delayed the execution of the mosaics.
73. RA R40/39; PP Windsor 527. The Crown Princess undertook to consider a design for this scheme, RA R40/34 and 35.
74. RA R40/39; PP Windsor 527A.
75. RA PP Windsor 527C.
76. RA PP Windsor 526A.

    Scott had proposed that the frescoes should be executed by John Rogers Herbert: G.G. Scott (ed.), *Personal and Professional Recollections by the late Sir George Gilbert Scott, R.A.*, London, 1879, p. 272. Scott probably chose frescoes for the walls in honour of Prince Albert's efforts to promote the medium in England, for which see M.H. Port (ed.), *The Houses of Parliament*, New Haven and London, 1976, pp. 268-81, and Marcia Pointon, *William Dyce 1806-1864. A critical biography*, Oxford, 1979.
77. RA R40/40.
78. RA R40/41.
79. RA PP Windsor 526; R40/31, 43, 44.
80. J. and M. Davison, *op. cit.*, introduction.
81. *Art Journal*, 1874, p. 368.
82. As note 80.
83. Triqueti's original scheme was for medallions of the Queen and her nine children. Queen Victoria asked, however, for reliefs of the Princess of Wales and of the Prince Consort to be included, the latter, with her own, to be placed over the entrance to the chapel (RA R40/43, 44). Although the medallion of the Princess of Wales replaced the Queen's, one of Prince Albert was not added. However, Susan Durant later executed reliefs of the Prince and the Queen, set in a single frame, which is now at Osborne.
84. Many letters written by Susan Durant at this time are preserved in the Royal Archives, together with her journal and

that of Emma Wallis, her companion on some of her visits to Osborne and Windsor. RA Vic Add. X/2 212.

85. RA Vic Add. X/2 212/A, Susan Durant's journal, 10 November 1865; Susan Durant to her father, 7 December 1865. The models for the medallions were acquired by Queen Victoria, and are now at Osborne. Susan Durant also executed, at the Queen's command, the monument to Leopold I, King of the Belgians, originally in St. George's Chapel, Windsor, but now at Christ Church, Esher. Susan Durant became friends with the Crown Princess and she travelled to Germany in September 1865 to model a medallion of her for the Wolsey Chapel. The sculptor gave the Princess lessons in modelling, and there was even talk of setting up a joint studio. In 1869 when Susan Durant and Triqueti were both staying at Potsdam, the Crown Princess expressed a wish for them to design a chapel in the Friederickskirche to her son Sigismund who had died in 1866, and whose bust Durant had earlier executed. RA Vic Add. X/2 212.

86. RA PP Windsor 655.
87. RA Vic Add. X/2 212/D. Susan Durant to Emma Wallis, 22 March 1868.
88. G.G. Scott (ed.), *op. cit.*, pp. 272-3.
89. RA PP Windsor 658C.
90. RA PP Windsor 761E.
91. RA PP Windsor 791A.
92. RA PP Windsor 835E.
93. RA PP Windsor 826 d, e.
94. RA PP Windsor 829, 830.
95. RA Vic Add. X/2 212/A. Susan Durant to her father, December 1865.
96. Letter, undated, in the possession of Richard A. Scott Esq.
97. RA R40/42.
98. See N. Penny, *Church Monuments in Romantic England*, New Haven and London, 1977, chapter five; B. Kemp, *English Church Monuments*, London, 1980, pp. 150-8.
99. A.W.N. Pugin, *An Apology for the Revival of Christian Architecture in England*, London, 1843, p. 34.
100. RA R40/42.
101. RA R40/45.
102. This model, together with those for all Triqueti's sculptures for the Wolsey Chapel, is in the Musée Girodet, Montargis, France.
103. RA PP Windsor 740.
104. RA PP Windsor 790.
105. *Art Journal*, 1872, p. 291.
106. RA PP Windsor 790.
107. RA PP Windsor 826.
108. *Art Journal*, 1874, p. 368.
109. RA PP Windsor 832; R40/72.
110. RA Queen Victoria's Journal, 4 July 1873.
111. RA R40/42. Scott had originally proposed that these niches should be filled with statues of Queen Victoria and Prince Albert in bronze. RA R40/6; undated letter from Queen Victoria to Scott in the possession of Richard A. Scott Esq.
112. These were completed by Joseph Edgar Boehm who was at this time executing the tomb of the Duke of Kent for St. George's Chapel. Boehm was also responsible for the tympanum depicting *The Entombment of Christ* over the west door: it is not clear whether this had been proposed by Triqueti, or was suggested after the sculptor's death.
113. RA Queen Victoria's Journal, 11 July 1874.
114. RA R40/75, Blanche Lee Childe (Triqueti's daughter) to the Dean of Windsor, 17 May 1874.

115. *Hour*, 23 June 1873, p. 5.
116. *Morning Post*, 2 December 1875, pp. 5-6.

NOTES TO CHAPTER THREE

1. *Survey of London*, chapter x, is a closely documented account of the monument upon which we have relied extensively for details of its history. See also S. Bayley, *The Albert Memorial: the monument in its social and architectural context*, London, 1981.
2. G.G. Scott (ed.), *Personal and Professional Recollections by the late Sir George Gilbert Scott, R.A.*, London, 1879, p. 225.
3. N.C. Smith, 'Mediaeval Monuments and Modern Heroes', unpublished Ph.D. thesis submitted to the University of Manchester, 1979.
4. *Builder*, viii, 1850, p. 43. Scott's design for the monument to William Duncombe, second Lord Feversham, put up in Helmsley, North Yorkshire, in 1869 is closely derived from the Bentinck Memorial. Furthermore, both monuments are in market places—and it is not surprising to discover that Duncombe was noted for his advocacy of agricultural protection.
5. *Manchester Examiner and Times*, 7 January 1862. *Builder*, xx, 1862, p. 28.
6. Manchester Central Reference Library, Archives Department (hereafter Manchester Archives), M 145/1/4/1.
7. *Builder*, xx, 1862, pp. 66-7, referring to Bishop Lee's plan for a memorial 'which he knew to have been felt by his Royal Highness himself to be a great want of the people of Manchester'.
8. *Ibid.*, p. 99.
9. Noble was an obvious choice. He had made his name with the Wellington monument erected in Manchester in 1856, and he had executed busts of the Prince Consort (1859) and Queen Victoria (1856) for the City Hall there.
10. Having discovered that it was much cheaper to carve the ornamental detail before the stonework was fixed in position, Worthington included in a revised design 'much more of this class of detail' than he had at first proposed (Manchester Archives, M 145/1/2/29). The changes he made include the addition of four nodding ogee arches to the base of the spire, and the enriching of the pinnacles and the motif at the centre of the main gable on each side. Further changes made for reasons of taste rather than as a result of the proposed economy included the type of decoration on the mouldings between the granite columns supporting the main arches, and the adoption of light stripes on a darker spire, a reversal of the original plan.
11. *Building News*, ix, 1862, p. 238.
12. *Builder*, xxi, 1863, p. 6.
13. Manchester Archives, M 145/1/2/53. The contractors were J.R. and E. Williams of Lombard Street, Manchester, and Joseph Bonehill undertook the carving. The only non-local firm employed on the monument was Skidmore's of Coventry who executed the wrought-iron gate—although the Manchester firm of Hibbert and Co. were responsible for the metal work of the terminal corona and the lightning conductor.
14. Many of the figures had to be re-carved during the recent restoration of the Manchester Albert Memorial. Some were missing and others badly damaged (*The Restoration of Manchester's Albert Memorial 1977/78: A Report of the Albert Memorial Appeal Committee*, printed in Manchester, 1979).
15. Manchester Archives, MISC 458.

16. Thomas Worthington, 'Memories', unpublished typescript reminiscences.
17. *The National Memorial to His Royal Highness The Prince Consort*, London, 1873 (hereafter *National Memorial*), p. 2.
18. *Ibid.*, pp. 3–4.
19. The search for a suitable stone went as far as Russian Finland—but Scottish granite was considered the most durable.
20. RA Queen Victoria's Journal, 4 April 1862.
21. RA Add. H1/283, mentioned in *Survey of London*, p. 150.
22. *National Memorial*, p. 10.
23. *Ibid.*, p. 10.
24. *Builder*, xxi, 1863, p. 233.
25. Scott's design was the only one to be published. Some of the coloured drawings submitted by Donaldson, Hardwick and Charles Barry survive in the R.I.B.A. Drawings Collection and Pennethorne's layout plan is to be found in the Public Record Office.
26. *Survey of London*, p. 152.
27. RA Add. I/17A, reprinted in the *Builder*, xxi, 1863, pp. 276–7, and quoted in *Survey of London*, p. 151.
28. In January 1863 it was even suggested that the monument to Sir Walter Scott in Edinburgh 'might at first glance be mistaken for one of the memorials to Eleanor, so nearly are some of the principal characteristics of that interesting series of monuments imitated in the modern work' (*Builder*, xxi, 1863, p. 6).
29. *Civil Engineer and Architect's Journal*, 1 April 1862, p. 94.
30. J. Abel, *Memorials of Queen Eleanor, illustrated by Photography: with a short account of their history and present condition*, London, 1864, foreword.
31. *Builder*, xxi, 1863, pp. 6, 233.
32. As note 27.
33. *Survey of London*, p. 153.
34. G.G. Scott (ed.), *op. cit.*, p. 263.
35. *Builder*, xxxi, 1873, p. 869. See also pp. 870, 912; xxxii, 1874, pp. 14–15. *Art Journal*, xii, 1873, p. 319. R.P.Pullen, *The Altar, its Baldachin and Reredos*, London, 1873. A.E. Street, *Memoir of George Edmund Street, R.A., 1824–1881*, London, 1888, pp. 71–4.
36. *Builder*, xxi, 1863, p. 6.
37. *National Memorial*, pp. 37–8.
38. He relied on details from the church of St. Mary, Nantwich, of which he had made measured drawings when he was a pupil in the office of Henry Bowman, and from the chapel of Sta. Maria della Spina in Pisa which he visited in 1848, later remarking that 'the richness and beauty of its detail induced me to make a study of it, parts of which in after years found their way into the Albert Memorial in Albert Square' (Thomas Worthington, 'Memories').
39. *The Works of John Ruskin* (eds. E.T. Cook and A. Wedderburn), 39 vols., London, 1903–12, x, p. 112; xxv, p. 491; xxiv, p. 414 (*Stones of Venice*, II, iv, §46; *Praeterita*, III, i, §19; *Circular respecting Memorial Studies of St. Mark's Venice*). See also N.C. Smith, 'Imitation and Invention in two Albert Memorials', *Burlington Magazine*, April 1981, pp. 232–6.
40. RA Add. H2/515 (proof copy) and Add. H2/519–24 (final version), discussed in S. Bayley, *op. cit.*, pp. 46–50. There is also a copy in the Victoria and Albert Museum.
41. RA Add. H2/547–9.
42. After Eastlake's death at the end of 1865 he was replaced by Henry Layard.
43. G.G. Scott (ed.), *op. cit.*, p. 268.
44. Skidmore's work on the wrought-iron railing which originally surrounded the Manchester Albert Memorial was less satisfactory. The gilding was damaged considerably during the fixing, and 'the rain and the damp dirty condition of the atmosphere' made it difficult to repair, because the gilding lost its brilliancy before it was set (Manchester Archives, M 145/1/3/55). The grille has been removed.
45. Farmer and Brindley were responsible for the plaster model of the Albert Memorial made for the Queen's approval in 1863, and now in the Victoria and Albert Museum.
46. *Builder*, xxi, 1863, p. 361.
47. *Builder*, xxxv, 1877, pp. 450, 452. The glasshouse was also intended to contain gardens representing the horticulture of the four quarters of the globe.
48. RA Add. H2/2035, quoted in *Survey of London*, p. 161.
49. John Bell took advantage of the situation to press his own idea for a kneeling figure of the prince, but this came to nothing. Illustrations of his design are published in S. Bayley, *op. cit.*, p. 62.
50. *Survey of London*, p. 162.
51. The gilding was removed during the First World War.
52. *National Memorial*, p. 36.
53. *Ibid.*, p. 47.
54. Scott felt that a better result might have been achieved had he 'exercised a stronger influence on the sculptors' (G.G. Scott (ed.), *op. cit.*, p. 266).
55. *National Memorial*, p. 59.
56. *Saturday Review*, 13 July 1872, p. 51.
57. *Survey of London*, p. 168.
58. *National Memorial*, p. 48.
59. RA Add. 1/17A, reprinted in the *Builder*, xxi, 1863, pp. 276–7, and quoted in *Survey of London*, p. 163. See also F. Haskell, *Rediscoveries in Art*, London, 1976, Chapter I.
60. RA Add. H2/821, Scott to Grey, quoted in *Survey of London*, p. 163.
61. Armstead's notebooks survive in the Royal Academy.
62. He is identified there as Arnolfo di Lapo—the other name by which he was then known.
63. RA Add. H2/675; Victoria and Albert Museum, 'Notes of German Tour by Henry Cole', 1863, p. 44; quoted in *Survey of London*, p. 158.
64. *National Memorial*, p. 47.
65. *Ibid.*, p. 47. The topmost part of the monument was damaged during the Second World War and, afterwards, the Ministry of Works replaced the cross facing the wrong way—north-south instead of east-west. A half-destroyed face from one of the damaged angels is preserved in the Royal Mausoleum at Frogmore—a poignant reminder of the Blitz.
66. *Art Pictorial and Industrial*, May 1871, p. 262.
67. *Pall Mall Gazette*, 5 July 1872, p. 10.
68. *Civil Engineer and Architect's Journal*, 1 August 1863, p. 220.
69. *Morning Advertiser*, 25 April 1863, p. 4.
70. *Saturday Review*, 13 July 1872, p. 51.
71. *Athenaeum*, 15 February, 15 November 1873, pp. 211, 633–4.
72. *The Times*, 14 November 1873, p. 3.
73. *Builder*, xxxi, 1873, pp. 917–18.
74. Manchester Archives, M 145/1/2/5. The proposal was not carried out in Dublin.
75. *Builder*, xxxii, 1874, p. 499, describes Chamberlain's design.
76. *Birmingham Gazette*, 28 April 1868. The surplus of the subscription fund led to the commission of a statue of Queen Victoria, which with the figure of Prince Albert was moved to a site at the top of the grand staircase in Birmingham Council House, to mark the Queen's Golden Jubilee.

NOTES TO CHAPTER FOUR

1. *Athenaeum*, 10 August 1850, p. 836.
2. *Cambridge Chronicle and University Journal*, 15 February 1862, p. 8.
3. *Glasgow Citizen*, 8 February 1862, p. 8.
4. *The Times*, 13 March 1862, p. 8.
5. *Building News*, ix, 1862, p. 195.
6. Thomas Carlyle, 'Hudson's Statue', *Latter-day Pamphlets*, London, 1850, p. 10.
7. Samuel Smiles, *Self Help*, 2nd edition, London, 1866, pp. 366–7.
8. *Birmingham Journal*, 25 January 1862, p. 6.
9. *The Times*, 6 September 1864, p. 7.
10. *British Workman*, February 1862, quoted in W.T. Kime, *Albert the Good*, London, 1862, part vi, pp. 29–30.
11. The Company also voted £100 towards the National Memorial, and re-named its new drill hall 'The Albert Room' in memory of the Prince Consort; it is still known by that name. Captain G.A. Raikes, *The History of the Honourable Artillery Company*, 2 vols., London, 1879, i, pp. 407–8.
12. Clothworkers' Company records, *Minutes of Court*, 5 February, 5 March 1862; *Minutes of General Superintendence Committee*, 19 March, 23 April, 11, 18 June, 30 July 1862, 29 July 1863 (information kindly supplied by the archivist, D.E. Wickham). *Art Journal*, 1863, p. 83.
13. RA PP Vic 21209 (March 1866), 23295 (December 1866), 23568 (April 1867); R. Ormond, *Early Victorian Portraits*, 2 vols., London, 1973, i, pp. 8–9.

    Queen Victoria also presented a three-quarter length portrait of Prince Albert in full-dress uniform to the 11th Hussars in 1866 'as a token of his affection for the Regiment'. The Prince Consort was Colonel of the Regiment which had been re-named Prince Albert's Own Hussars in 1840. The painting hangs in the Officers' Mess at Winchester (information kindly supplied by Lieutenant Colonel P.K. Upton, Regimental Secretary, The Royal Hussars).
14. *Journal of the Society of Arts*, xi, 13 February, 24 July 1863; Sir Henry Trueman Wood, *A History of the Royal Society of Arts*, London, 1913, pp. 80, 399–400; W. Pressly, 'James Barry's proposed extensions for his Adelphi series', Part i, *Journal of the Royal Society of Arts*, cxliv, March 1978, pp. 233–7.
15. *Reminiscences of Charles West Cope R.A.* by his son, Charles Henry Cope, M.A., London, 1891, p. 254.
16. *A series of etchings by James Barry, Esq., from his original and justly celebrated paintings, in the Great Room of the Society of Arts, Manufactures, and Commerce, Adelphi*, London, 1808.
17. The medal records that Prince Albert was President of the Society from 1842 until 1861. In fact, he was elected President on 26 May 1843, following the death of the Duke of Sussex in April. The Albert Medal was awarded to Queen Victoria in the year of her Golden Jubilee, 1887.
18. *Catalogue of Sculpture, Paintings, Engravings, and other works of Art belonging to the Corporation, together with books not included in the Catalogue of the Guildhall Library*, 2 vols., London, 1867–8, i, p. 6; *Builder*, xx, 1862, pp. 155, 555; *Art Journal*, 1862, p. 195; *Athenaeum*, 15 February 1862, p. 228. The Lord Provost of Edinburgh presented a bust of Prince Albert by Theed, and one of Queen Victoria by Matthew Noble, to the Council Chamber in 1864. (*Building News*, xi, 1864, p. 668.)
19. *Builder*, xx, 1862, p. 112.
20. *Illustrated London News*, 6 June 1863, pp. 613, 622. We are grateful to Dr. Edward Diestelkamp for drawing our attention to this.
21. *Athenaeum*, 19 July 1862, p. 85. The medallion has been lost and has been replaced by a portrait of the Prince commissioned in 1873. (Information kindly provided by I.H. Blenkinsop, Secretary of the Royal Statistical Society.) Another plaster medallion of Prince Albert by Butler is in the Royal College of Physicians, London.
22. *Ibid.*, 17 January 1863, p. 88. See also 25 October 1862, p. 531; *Building News*, ix, 1862, p. 344, x, 1863, p. 70; *Art Journal*, 1862, p. 238. The bust remained in the front hall until 1964 when the building was altered, and is now lost.
23. RA PP2/99/9673.
24. Alderman Sir J.J. Baddeley, Bt., J.P., *The Guildhall of the City of London*, seventh edition, London, 1939, p. 55.
25. RA PP Vic 5966 (December 1869); L26/23, 24, 26; Vic Add. A17/39.
26. T.P. Cooper, *A Guide to the Guildhall of the City of York*, York, 1909, pp. 42–3. A window showing Prince Albert surrounded by emblems representing engineering, sculpture, architecture, commerce, manufacture and agriculture, by Heaton, Butler and Bayne, was placed opposite one of Queen Victoria in the Assembly Room of Rochdale Town Hall in the 1860s. M.L. Maxim, *Rochdale Town Hall*, Rochdale, 1959, p. 50.
27. *The memorial window in St. George's Chapel, Windsor; its spirit and details by one of the Chapter*, Eton, 1863, p. 22. See also Rodney Hubbuck, 'Curiosities in English Stained Glass 1837–1914', *Journal of the British Society of Master Glass-Painters*, vol. xvi, nos. 2, 3, 1979–80. A window by Wailes showing Prince Albert in his robes as Chancellor of Cambridge University, together with one of Queen Victoria, had been placed in Ely Cathedral in 1857, but in the Octagon.
28. RA R4/109. Other stained glass windows in memory of Prince Albert can be found at Christchurch, Banbury, 1863, by T. Drury of Warwick; St. Peter, Chester, 1862, and St. Michael, Coventry, both by Heaton, Butler and Bayne; All Saints, Derby (now Cathedral), 1863, and Abbey Church, Malvern, both by Clayton and Bell; St. John, Eton, 1865, and St. Mary, Datchet, 1862, both by O'Connor of London; Christchurch, Harpurhey, Greater Manchester, 1862, by Edmundson and Son; Low Harrogate Church, Harrogate, 1862, by John Knowles; St. Michael, Highworth (Wiltshire), 1862, by Wailes of Newcastle; Trinity Church, Knaresborough, (North Yorkshire), 1862, St. Mary Magdalen, Newark (Nottinghamshire), 1864, and St. John, Yeovil, 1863, all by Hardman and Co. (the last with a tiled floor by Minton's incorporating the Prince's coats of arms); St. Botolph, Northfleet (Kent), 1862; St. Martin-on-the-Hill, Scarborough, 1862 (the gift of Mary Craven), by Morris, Marshall, Faulkner and Co.; St. Peter, Walworth, 1863, by Ward and Hughes.
29. *The memorial window in St. George's Chapel, Windsor; its spirit and details by one of the Chapter*, Eton, 1863, p. 27.
30. RA R4/71.
31. *The memorial window in St. George's Chapel, Windsor; its spirit and details by one of the Chapter*, Eton, 1863, pp. 17, 29–30. The reredos beneath the window, designed by G.G. Scott and with sculpture executed by J.B. Philip, also formed part of the memorial to Prince Albert.
32. RA Y109/20.
33. *Builder*, xx, 1862, pp. 445, 934.
34. *Ibid.*, pp. 227, 241, 276, 292, 483, 916.
35. *Ibid.*, pp. 210–11.
36. *Proceedings at a meeting of the central committee for promoting the Scottish National Memorial to the late Prince Consort held at*

Edinburgh March 19, 1862, Edinburgh, 1862.

37. Scottish Record Office, GD 224 666/3, Report of the Sub-committee of the Scottish National Memorial Fund, 20 January 1863.

38. *Ibid.*, W.S. Walker (Hon. Sec. of the Committee) to Buccleuch, 19 May 1863; Sir W. Gibson-Craig to Buccleuch, 12 December 1863; memorandum of correspondence with Paton; memorandum of meeting, 9 July 1863. RA Add. I/27, 28, 46, 47. Paton's design does not appear to have survived, but it is illustrated in *Art Journal*, 1895, p. 114.

39. Scottish Record Office, GD 224 666/3, Grey to Buccleuch, 3 March 1865. Sixty designs were submitted in competition and of these, six were sent to Queen Victoria in February 1865 for her final selection. The other designs shown to her were by J.N. Paton; by David Bryce for an Albert Keep; by W.C. Marshall for a statue surmounting a column with additional statuary; by Joseph Durham and John Robinson for a statue on a column with four seated angels at the base; and by Steell for another equestrian statue on a Gothic pedestal in the form of a cairn. RA Add. I/105, 110, 114–17; *Catalogue of designs for the Scottish National Memorial to H.R.H. the Prince Consort*, Edinburgh, December 1864.

40. RA Add. I/171. Excerpt from minutes of Executive Committee meeting, 2 July 1870.

41. RA Add. I/170.

42. RA Add. I/176.

43. Scottish Record Office, GD 224 666/3, excerpt from minutes of Executive Committee meeting, 12 July 1871; RA Add. I/184. See also Rev. D. Aitkin's diary, *The Book of the Old Edinburgh Club*, xxxiii, 1971, pp. 61–95.

44. Scottish Record Office, GD 224 666/3, excerpts from minutes of Executive Committee meetings, 1 July 1868, 2 August 1869; minutes of meetings, 8, 20 May 1872; Walker to Buccleuch, 9 March, 11 May 1872, 16 August 1873. RA Add. I/148, 152, 153, 192, 203, 204, 207.

45. Scottish Record Office, GD 224 666/3, Walker to Buccleuch, 30 March 1874. RA Add. I/227.

46. Scottish Record Office, GD 224 666/3, Walker to Buccleuch, 14 September 1875.

47. The bust for the statue was modelled life-size during the summer of 1865 under Queen Victoria's supervision at Windsor Castle where the sculptor was given access to photographs, drawings and paintings of the Prince Consort. He was also lent the Field Marshal's uniform to copy. RA Add. I/137, 138, 140, 145; *Illustrated London News*, 26 August 1876, p. 187. Queen Victoria approved the general effect of the completed monument, but privately expressed some dissatisfaction with the figure of Prince Albert, and especially with the horse which she thought was 'not good'. Nonetheless, because Steell was 'such a kind, good man with a good deal of talent', she conferred a knighthood on him after the unveiling, and commissioned a marble version of the bust of Prince Albert for the Royal Collection. R. Fulford (ed.), *Darling Child: Private Correspondence of Queen Victoria and the Crown Princess of Prussia 1871–1878*, London, 1976, p. 221; RA Add. I/239.

48. *Scotsman*, 11 March 1865, p. 2.

49. *Ibid.*, 1 August 1876, p. 3.

50. Long quotations from Prince Albert's speeches were to have been cut into the pedestal on all sides below these emblems, but they were omitted in the final work. They appear in an undated drawing in the Royal Archives, Add. I/18.

51. The group of the labouring classes was originally entrusted to George MacCallum but, following his death in August 1868,

it passed to D.W. Stevenson, together with the group of the Arts and Education. John Hutchison was contracted initially for the latter group, but he rejected the commission on the grounds that the remuneration was inadequate. It was then offered to Brodie, who declined it, whereupon Steell undertook it himself. As he was already executing the equestrian statue and the bas-reliefs, and supervising the casting of all the bronze work in his foundry, he took the opportunity of later consigning this group to D.W. Stevenson. All the sculptors worked from sketch models prepared by Steell.

52. *Scotsman*, 11 March 1865, p. 2.

53. *Ibid.*

54. Scottish Record Office, GD 224 666/3, Grey to Buccleuch, 3 March 1865.

55. *Irish Times*, 17 March 1862; *Dublin Builder*, iv, 1862, p. 260.

56. *Builder*, xx, 1862, p. 719; *Dublin Builder*, v, 1863, p. 101.

57. *Dublin Builder*, vi, 1864, p. 70.

58. *Ibid.*, v, 1863, p. 3.

59. RA PP Vic 20663, December 1865.

60. RA D27/100.

61. *Irish Times*, 5 June 1872, p. 5.

62. *Dublin Daily Express*, 11 June 1872; *Morning Mail*, 11 June 1872. The memorial has been moved from a central position to a site by the museum.

63. *Tenby and Pembroke Dock Observer*, 7 January 1864.

64. *Ibid.*, 7 July 1864.

65. *An account of the Welsh Memorial erected to His Royal Highness the Prince Consort as a mark of loyalty to Her Most Gracious Majesty the Queen, and of affectionate respect and gratitude to the memory of Albert the Good*, Tenby, 1866, p. 24.

66. *Glasgow Citizen*, 1 March 1862, p. 3.

67. *Builder*, xxi, 1863, p. 504.

68. *Glasgow Citizen*, 25 July 1863, p. 9.

69. *Wolverhampton Chronicle*, 19 November 1862, p. 4.

70. Liverpool Record Office, 352 MIN/SPE 1/2, pp. 103–4, letter from Thomas Thornycroft, 4 December 1862.

71. *Illustrated London News*, 20 October 1866, p. 376.

72. The *Wolverhampton Chronicle* (26 March 1862, p. 4), believed that Thornycroft could be relied upon to produce a 'faithful representation' for this reason, and the *Halifax Courier* (15 November 1862, p. 5) pointed out that 'a long personal knowledge of the Prince' had enabled Thornycroft to 'catch a very excellent likeness' in his sketch model for the town's memorial.

73. It was removed to Heath Park (re-named Albert Park), at the junction of Skircoat Road and Heath Road, in 1900.

74. *Illustrated London News*, 8 December 1866, p. 562.

75. *Building News*, xiii, 1866, p. 804.

76. *Morning Journal*, 19 October 1866, p. 2. The statue was unveiled on 18 October 1866.

77. *Tenby and Pembroke Dock Observer*, 3 March 1864.

78. *Ibid.* Electrotypes were casts of pure copper which were formed by the action of a galvanic battery. The technique had been developed in England in the 1840s by Elkington's of Birmingham, initially for small, decorative items, and was one in which Prince Albert took a keen interest. The process seems to have been applied to large-scale statuary from the late 1850s, the figures of the memorial to the Great Exhibition being early examples. S. Timmins (ed.), *The Resources, Products, and Industrial History of Birmingham and the Midland Hardware District*, London, 1866, pp. 510–19; S. Bury, *Victorian Electroplate*, London, 1971.

79. *The Times*, 30 August 1865, p. 9.

80. RA Y114/30. The statue was cast in bronze from cannon donated by Queen Victoria's uncle, King Leopold and King William of Prussia, the Crown Princess's father-in-law. The corporation of Coburg furnished the pedestal. *Illustrated London News*, 16 September 1865, p. 270.

81. RA R4/77.

82. The statue is now in the Botanic Gardens, Sydney.

83. The statue was unveiled on 22 July 1879 by the Prince and Princess of Wales and is now in front of the Dock Offices in Grimsby. It was intended to commemorate the opening of the Union Dock built by the Manchester, Sheffield and Lincolnshire Railway of which Sir E. W. Watkin was Chairman. This linked the old dock with the Royal Dock, the foundation stone of which had been laid by Prince Albert in 1849. For this reason, the plan of the Great Exhibition which the Prince holds in Theed's Coburg statue, was replaced by one of the Grimsby Docks in this version.

84. This figure was made at the terracotta works of J.M. Blashfield in part from clay from the estate of Arthur Helps. It was moved to outside God's House Tower in Southampton in 1876 following the closure of Bishop's Waltham Infirmary. In 1907 it was placed in store for fear its delapidated state might offend Kaiser Wilhelm II during his visit to Southampton, and it was broken up during the First World War. *Builder*, xxiii, 1865, pp. 709-10; *Illustrated London News*, 18 November 1865, p. 478; *Southampton Observer*, 26 February 1876; Robert Douch, *Monuments and Memorials in Southampton*, Southampton papers no. 6, 1968, p. 40.

85. Andrew Murray, *The Book of the Royal Horticultural Society 1862-1863*, London, 1963, p. 67.

86. RA Y109/34.

87. *Birmingham Journal*, 31 May 1862, p. 3.

88. Replicas of Durham's statue were also suggested at Tenby (*Tenby and Pembroke Dock Observer*, 3 March 1864) and at Halifax (*Halifax Guardian*, 7 June 1862, p. 4). In 1863 Durham also sought Queen Victoria's permission to present a cast to Alexandra Palace in London, an idea which General Grey supported, adding that he considered 'Your Majesty will not think this statue can be too widely reproduced.' RA R4/97.

89. S.M. Ellis (ed.), *A Mid-Victorian Pepys. The Letters and Memoirs of Sir William Hardman, M.A., F.R.G.S.*, London, 1923, p. 203.

90. *Builder*, 12 August 1864, p. 621.

91. *Perthshire Courier*, 13 October 1863.

92. *Ibid.*, 22 December 1863.

93. *Tenby and Pembroke Dock Observer*, 28 July 1864.

94. The committee had selected 'the classical model' from those submitted by Foley at a meeting on 21 February 1865. Cambridge University Archives, University Library, 0.1.14.

95. RA Add. U/32, 7 December 1867. Queen Victoria observed in this letter to the Crown Princess that Foley 'is a man of gt. genius & talent & dearest Papa admired him so much'.

96. Charles Summers's statue of Prince Albert, presented by Sir W.J. Clarke to the National Gallery of Victoria, Melbourne in 1879 (together with figures of Queen Victoria and the Prince and Princess of Wales), also shows him in Chancellor's robes. The statue is now at the showgrounds of the Royal Agricultural Society of Victoria at Melbourne.

97. The Victoria Museum, Bombay, was re-named the Victoria and Albert Museum after the Prince Consort's death. The statue, which cost £3,000, was the gift of David Sassoon, and the commission was probably given to Noble because he was already executing a figure of the Queen for the Victoria Gardens there. Similarly, Noble had already executed statues of the Queen for Salford and Leeds when he was commissioned for the memorial figures of Prince Albert.

98. *Times of India*, 4 May 1872, pp. 2-3.

99. RA R4/77. Queen Victoria rejected a suggestion from the Duke of Newcastle that Noble should execute the statue of the Prince Consort for Sydney, and the sculptor was excluded from working on the National Memorial because she had a low opinion of his work. RA Add. H2/785; *Survey of London*, p. 165.

100. *Civil Engineer and Architect's Journal*, March 1840, p. 86.

101. *The Times*, 10 August 1864, p. 8.

102. *The Times*, 6 August 1864, p. 6.

103. *Manchester Guardian*, 8 November 1864, p. 6.

104. *Midland Counties Herald*, 30 April 1868, p. 71.

105. F.T. Palgrave, 'Public Statues in London', *Broadway*, March 1868, p. 526.

106. F.T. Palgrave, *Essays on Art*, London and Cambridge, 1866, pp. 123-4.

107. *Morning Advertiser*, 10 August 1864, p. 3. The statue was originally erected in the grounds of the Association's Asylum in Kennington, but is now in its garden village at Denham, Buckinghamshire.

108. *Hull and North Lincolnshire Times*, 17 October 1868, pp. 6-7. Earle's original proposal to place a statue of Prince Albert with the one of Victoria he was already executing on a single pedestal was approved by the Committee but rejected by the Queen, and consequently was abandoned in favour of a separate figure. *Ibid.*, 18 January 1868, p. 2.

109. Quoted in the *Oxford Times*, 9 April 1864, p. 6.

110. *Aberdeen Herald*, 17 October 1863, p. 5.

111. *Aberdeen Journal*, 21 October 1863, p. 8.

112. *Aberdeen Free Press*, 16 October 1863, p. 5.

113. *Ibid.*; *Aberdeen Herald*, 17 October 1863, p. 8. Brodie's statue was to have been based on John Phillip's painting of Prince Albert in Highland dress.

114. The other two are Foley's statue for the National Memorial, and Charles Summers's figure at Melbourne. Marochetti's statue cost approximately £3,000.

115. RA Y110/18.

116. RA R4/78.

117. *Dearest Mama*, p. 273.

NOTES TO CHAPTER FIVE

1. *Saturday Review*, 11 June 1870, quoted in *Survey of London*, p. 185.

2. *Builder*, xx, 1862, p. 318.

3. *A Guide to the Art Collections of the South Kensington Museum*, 1868, p. 36; *Survey of London*, p. 110; John Physick, *The Victoria and Albert Museum. The History of its Building*, London, 1982, pp. 69-71. The Gallery was to have included portraits of Queen Victoria and the royal Princes and Princesses but these were not executed. The Gallery is now a store, but the portrait of Prince Albert is still visible in Room 102.

4. G.T. Donisthorpe, *An account of the origin and progress of the Devon and Exeter Albert Memorial Museum*, Exeter, 1868; *Builder*, xx, 1862, p. 155; xxii, 1864, pp. 337-8, 414-15, 477, 499; *Art Journal*, 1863, p. 17; 1865, p. 371; 1869, p. 288. The Royal Albert Memorial College is now incorporated in University College, Exeter. An Albert Museum, to become part of the Plymouth Institution, was proposed in that town in

1862, but it did not materialise, probably because the museum in Exeter drew subscriptions from the whole county.

5. In 1880 a statue of Prince Albert by Romanelli was presented to the Institute by Mrs. Richardson-Gardner, whose husband donated an identical figure six years later. Both were restored and incorporated into the redevelopment of the site, completed in 1977, and named Royal Albert House.

6. It was also proposed to erect 'a grand pyramid' in memory of the Prince on Worlebury Hill, Weston-super-Mare, but this was not carried out. *Builder*, xxi, 1863, p. 777; *Art Journal*, 1863, p. 246.

7. F.A. Johnson, *The proposed Scientific College for Suffolk, shewn to be a Necessity, and the carrying out of the National Designs of His late Royal Highness, with the reasons why it should be generally supported*, London, 1862; J. Booth, *Framlingham College: The First Sixty Years*, Ipswich, 1925. See also *Builder*, xx, 1862, pp. 227, 259, 318; xxi, 1863, p. 601; xxii, 1864, pp. 80-3; *Art Journal*, 1864, p. 282; *Illustrated London News*, 18 May 1867, p. 488. We are grateful to Mr. L. Gillett, Librarian of Framlingham College, for pointing out much of this material.

Less ambitious undertakings in memory of the Prince Consort in Suffolk also reflected the county's concern for education. In Ipswich an Albert scholarship was founded in 1862 at Queen Elizabeth's Grammar School, the foundation stone of which had been laid by Prince Albert in 1851 (*Ipswich Journal*, 6 April 1862, p. 6. See also *Builder*, xx, 1862, pp. 48, 135, 155, 259.)

8. *Life of Sir William Jackson, Bart.* (reprinted from the *Liverpool Mercury*), 1876, pp. 21-4; J. Kaighin, *Bygone Birkenhead*, Birkenhead, 1925, p. 197; E. Hubbard and N. Pevsner, *Cheshire*, Harmondsworth, 1971, p. 85. Before deciding in favour of the school, Jackson had proposed to present a statue of Prince Albert, to be erected in Birkenhead Park (see *Builder*, xx, 1862, p. 99).

9. Its commemorative origin seems to have been quickly forgotten. S.G. Jarman, *A History of Bridgwater*, London, 1889, does not mention it.

10. *Bridgwater Mercury*, 12 July 1865. See also *Builder*, xx, 1862, pp. 189, 348, 555.

11. *Builder*, xx, 1862, p. 318.

12. The infirmary was built on land given by Sir Arthur Helps who devoted the profits from the sale of his *Principal Speeches and Addresses of His Royal Highness the Prince Consort* towards its establishment. After his death in 1875, the building was claimed by his creditors and sold as a private house. It was taken over by the White Fathers in 1912, and by the Police Cadets as a training school in April 1971 after it had stood empty for some time. *Builder*, xxiii, 1865, p. 767; *White's History, Gazetteer and Directory of the County of Hampshire*, 1878, p. 147; *Victoria County History of Hampshire*, III, London, 1908, p. 277; *Hampshire Treasures: Droxford Rural District* (Hampshire County Council draft report), July 1972, p. 8.

13. *Builder*, xx, 1862, pp. 292, 318; xxi, 1863, p. 567; A.J.B. Green, *A short history of the Royal Surrey County Hospital* (issued by the committee of management), 1948.

14. N. Pevsner, *North Lancashire*, Harmondsworth, 1969, p. 163. There is a statue of Prince Albert (and one of Queen Victoria) on the façade of the building.

15. *Sydney Morning Herald*, 25 April 1866, p. 2.

16. *Builder*, xx, 1862, pp. 136, 276; *Wakefield Journal and Examiner*, 6 November 1863; *Wakefield Express*, 7 November 1863. In 1876 Clayton Hospital was moved to a different site in Northgate, Wakefield. The 1863 building, which had a stone tablet on the wall recording its link with Prince Albert, was recently demolished.

17. *Bath United Hospital Annual Reports*, 1864, 1865, 1866 and *Bath Royal United Hospital Annual Report*, 1868; *Builder*, xx, 1862, pp. 136, 155, 189, 210; xxi, 1863, p. 175. In 1936 the hospital moved to its present site and the building was taken over by the City Council for use as a technical college. The name of Albert (and also that of Victoria) was perpetuated in the hospital, however, as two wards are named after them in the present building.

18. *Builder*, xx, 1862, p. 66; *Derbyshire Times*, 18 January, 22 February 1862.

19. *Building News*, x, 1863, pp. 834-5.

20. *Builder*, xx, 1862, p. 155; xxi, 1863, p. 122; and information kindly supplied by the Gravesend Divisional Librarian. A road in Gravesend was also named Albert Place after the Prince Consort.

21. *Builder*, xx, 1862, p. 514; *Building News*, xii, 1865, p. 91.

22. RA PP Vic 1035, 1925, 3439.

23. Designed by John Lowe, the church was consecrated on 25 April 1864, but demolished in 1972. *English Churchman*, 17 June 1949; N. Pevsner, *South Lancashire*, Harmondsworth, 1969, p. 315.

24. *Stamford Mercury*, 4 March, 10 July 1863, 8 May 1874; *Builder*, xxi, 1863, p. 634.

25. It is possible that 'Albert' biscuits, produced by Huntley and Palmers, were also named after the Prince of Wales, as other biscuits were called after royal children. We are grateful to Anthony Corley and Michael Franklin for discussing this problem with us.

26. S. Gordon, *The Watering Places of Cleveland*, Redcar, 1869, p. 14; K. Hoole, *Forgotten Railways: North-East England*, 1973, pp. 117-18. It is shown in N. Bainbridge, *Saltburn-by-the-Sea: a pictorial history*, Redcar, 1977, plate 9.

27. *Builder*, xx, 1862, pp. 227-8, 719, 916; xxiii, 1865, p. 611; *Art Journal*, 1865, p. 312.

28. D. Lewer and J.B. Calkin, *The Curiosities of Swanage*, 1971, p. 7; *Builder*, xx, 1862, pp. 136, 155. The Albert obelisk in Swanage was recently removed from its position in the High Street to make room for new buildings. The main part of it is now in the yard of the Purbeck District Council, Court Hill, Swanage. A smaller portion is to be found at Lander's Quarries at nearby Worth Matravers.

29. *Wrexham Weekly Advertiser*, 23 September 1865. See also *Builder*, xxiii, 1865, p. 692; C.H. Leslie, *Rambles Round Mold*, 1869, p. 89. A lithograph of Mold published in 1874 by Pring and Price shows the fountain. This print was re-issued in 1976 by Clwyd County Council.

30. H.J. Tweddell, *Handy Guide to Mold and the Neighbourhood*, Mold, 1891, p. 23. The clock itself was saved and set up in front of the Town Hall, and the steps were removed to a public garden.

31. *Builder*, xx, 1862, pp. 170, 292, 348, 375, 846; xxi, 1863, pp. 169-70 (engraving), 513, 637; *Art Journal*, 1862, p. 238; 1863, p. 176; *Parsons' Guide to Hastings and St. Leonards*, Hastings, 1897, p. 26. In 1973 the monument was set on fire and so badly damaged that it had to be demolished. The statue of Prince Albert was salvaged and is now in a greenhouse in a local park.

32. *Builder*, xx, 1862, p. 483. At Rye, Sussex, an Albert clock was fixed in the Landgate in 1863. (*Builder*, xxi, 1863, p. 431.)

33. *Builder*, xx, 1862, pp. 190, 737; xxiii, 1865, pp. 447, 464, 487, 525, 539; xxiv, 1866, pp. 331, 374, 410; *Art Journal*, 1862, p.

223; 1865, p. 146; 1870, p. 86; *Dublin Builder*, vii, 1865, pp. 135, 153, 164, 183, 205-6, 214; viii, 1866, p. 117; xi, 1869, pp. 124, 183-6.

34. *Builder*, xx, 1862, p. 227. See also p. 241.

35. *Builder*, xx, 1862, p. 348; *Illustrated London News*, 6 February 1864. The fountain has been demolished.

36. F. Barrett, *A History of Queensbury*, 1963, pp. 37-8; A.H. Robinson, 'A Noble Recognition', *Band of Hope Chronicle*, January-February 1977.

37. *Belfast Newsletter*, 27 June 1865.

38. *The Times*, 17 December 1861, p. 7.

39. *The Weekly Register*, 21 December 1861.

40. S.M. Ellis (ed.), *A mid-Victorian Pepys: The Letters and Memoirs of Sir William Hardman, M.A., F.R.G.S.*, London, 1923, p. 69.

41. J.A.V. Chapple and Arthur Pollard (eds.), *The Letters of Mrs. Gaskell*, Manchester, 1966, p. 496.

42. *Lady's Newspaper and Pictorial Times*, 28 December 1861.

43. *The Queen*, 28 December 1861, pp. 340-2. The magazine also published patterns for memorial collars.

44. Derek Hudson, *Munby, Man of Two Worlds: The Life and Diaries of Arthur J. Munby 1828-1910*, London, 1974, p. 111.

45. *Notes and Queries*, second series, xii, 28 December 1861, p. 518.

46. Public Record Office, BT 43/397. Design registered April 1862, number 151136.

47. RA Add. A15/967.

48. Flora Thompson, *Lark Rise to Candleford*, Harmondsworth, 1973 (first published 1939-43), p. 295.

49. M. Darby, 'Victoria and Albert in silk', *Country Life*, 6 March 1969, pp. 546, 549-50. The Basle firm of Koechlin and Sons also produced a woven silk bookmark. A woven silk picture of the National Albert Memorial by Barlow and Jones Ltd., dated 1881, is in the Victoria and Albert Museum, Department of Textiles.

50. *Art Journal*, April 1862, p. 110.

51. O. Matthews, *The Album of Carte-de-Visite and Cabinet Portrait Photographs 1854-1914*, London, 1974, p. 52.

52. *Builder*, xx, 1862, p. 75.

53. *The Queen*, 11 January 1862, p. 365.

54. Derek Hudson, *op. cit.*, p. 111.

55. *Art Journal*, 1862, p. 241.

56. RA Queen Victoria's Journal, 27 May 1862. Other commemorative prints are listed in F. O'Donoghue, *Catalogue of Engraved British Portraits preserved in the Department of Prints and Drawings in the British Museum*, London, 1908. The National Portrait Gallery Archive also contains a number.

57. Robert Awde, *Waiting at Table. Poems and Songs*, London, 1865, pp. 21-31. The photograph is pasted into the front of the book, and another copy is to be found in S.M. Ellis (ed.), *op. cit.* The position of some of the figures in these photographs differs from those in the painting.

58. *The Last Hours of His Royal Highness Prince Albert of Blessed Memory*, London, 1864. *Illustrated Weekly Times*, 28 December 1861, p. 177, published its own illustration of the deathbed scene.

59. *The Times*, 16 December 1861, p. 9, recorded that Generals Grey and Seymour and Colonel Elphinstone were present, but they are not included in the picture, whereas Prince Arthur and the Princesses Louise and Beatrice, Major Teesdale and four physicians, Doctors Clark, Ferguson, Jenner and Watson, are represented although they are not mentioned in *The Times*.

60. RA PP Vic 23413 (March 1867).

61. National Portrait Gallery Archive; "*This Brilliant Year*": *Queen Victoria's Jubilee 1887*, catalogue of an exhibition held at the Royal Academy of Arts, London, 1977, no. 57.

62. See, for example, S.M. Ellis (ed.), *op. cit.*, p. 69; Hon. Mrs. Norton, 'Royal Deaths. The Princess and the Prince 1817-1861', *MacMillan's Magazine*, March 1862, pp. 441-51.

63. Some objects, such as the parian busts exhibited by Brown-Westhead, Moore and Co., and Minton and Co., and one in terracotta made by J.M. Blashfield, and vases by Bevington and Son and Wedgwood which incorporated portraits of Prince Albert, were not necessarily produced as commemorative items, but would have been manufactured anyway for such an occasion. Similarly, Thomas Thornycroft showed a marble bust of the Prince which was not necessarily executed in consequence of his death.

64. Public Record Office, BT 43/69. Design number 150538, registered 9 April 1862. C. and D. Shinn, *Victorian Parian China*, London, 1971, plate 87, illustrate a rare example in which the background to the medallion is coloured blue.

65. *Art Journal*, 1863, p. 120. An example is in the Swiss Cottage Museum, Osborne House.

66. See J. and J. May, *Commemorative Pottery 1780-1900*, London, 1972.

67. *Art Journal*, 1862, p. 211.

68. Public Record Office, BT 43/13. Design number 150094, registered by Charles Rowley & Co., 21 March 1862.

69. *Ibid.*, Design number 147951, registered by Edwin Green and Joel Cadbury, 26 December 1861.

70. *Ibid.*, Design number 149196, registered by Joseph Baker, 5 February 1862.

71. *Ibid.*, Design number 148742, registered by Jos. Litchfield, 22 January 1862.

72. *Ibid.*, BT 43/14. Design number 157955, registered by William Corbitt & Son, 29 November 1862.

73. *Art Journal*, 1862, p. 163 commended the portrait of Albert on the obverse as 'in extremely bold and sharp relief, yet free from all rigidity of expression'.

74. *Ibid.*, p. 62.

75. *Dearest Mama*, p. 64.

76. *Athenaeum*, 3 May 1862, p. 592.

77. R.C. Lehmann (ed.), *Charles Dickens as Editor, being letters written by him to William Henry Wills, his sub-editor*, London, 1912, pp. 300-1.

78. *Charles Dickens to John Leech*, privately printed by Walter Dexter, 1938, p. 42.

79. *Illustrated London News*, 24 October 1863, p. 414.

80. *Aberdeen Herald*, 10 October 1863, p. 5; *Aberdeen Journal*, 14 October 1863, p. 8.

81. RA M58/70, Y110/18.

82. *The Times*, 12 October 1863, p. 8.

83. RA Add.U/143, 2 September 1864.

84. RA Y114/30.

85. *The Times*, 30 August 1865, p. 8.

86. *Charles Dickens to John Leech*, privately printed by Walter Dexter, 1938, p. 42.

87. *The Times*, 30 August 1865, p. 8.

88. *Dearest Mama*, pp. 85-6.

89. British Library, Add. MS. 43765, Diary of Lord Broughton, xxii, 1862-3, f. 82.

90. Ursula Bloom, *Edward and Victoria*, London, 1977, p. 103.

91. British Library, Add. MS. 43765, f. 79.

92. *The Letters of Queen Victoria*, second series, edited by G.E. Buckle, 3 vols., London, 1926, i, pp. 74, 77.

93. Elizabeth Longford, *Victoria R.I.*, London, 1966, pp. 485–6; Kingsley Martin, *The Crown and the Establishment*, London, 1962, pp. 43–50.

94. Jeffrey L. Lant, *Insubstantial Pageant: Ceremony and Confusion at Queen Victoria's Court*, London, 1979, p. 26.

95. *Ibid.*, p. 32.

96. Flora Thompson, *op. cit.*, p. 239.

97. RA PP Vic Box G/16, Ponsonby to Hogg, 1 August 1886.

98. *Ibid.*, Knollys to Ponsonby, 9 December 1886.

99. *Ibid.*, Lady Cork to Ponsonby, 9 January 1887.

100. See also Jeffrey L. Lant, *op. cit.*, pp. 134–8, 146–9.

101. A group of Prince Albert and Queen Victoria was placed in the Storey Art Institute, Lancaster, in commemoration of the Golden Jubilee, for example, and another figure of the Prince, together with one of the Queen was put up on the façade of the Victoria and Albert Museum in 1907. Stained glass windows incorporating an image of Prince Albert include one at St. Stephen's, Bristol, erected *c.* 1901 and destroyed during the Second World War, which also contained a portrait of Queen Victoria, and one in Birmingham Law Courts, part of a series commissioned for the Golden Jubilee, which shows him laying the foundation stone of the Midland Institute. The Jubilee clock-tower at Brighton, unveiled in 1888, includes portraits of Queen Victoria, Prince Albert, and the Prince and Princess of Wales.

102. Flora Thompson, *op. cit.*, p. 295.

Index

119